Working Papers

for use with

Financial Accounting
Information for Decisions

Third Edition

John J. Wild
University of Wisconsin at Madison

McGraw-Hill Irwin

Boston Burr Ridge, IL Dubuque, IA Madison, WI New York San Francisco St. Louis Bangkok Bogotá Caracas Kuala Lumpur Lisbon London Madrid Mexico City Milan Montreal New Delhi Santiago Seoul Singapore Sydney Taipei Toronto

McGraw-Hill Irwin

Working Papers for use with
FINANCIAL ACCOUNTING: INFORMATION FOR DECISIONS
John J. Wild

Published by McGraw-Hill/Irwin, an imprint of The McGraw-Hill Companies, Inc., 1221 Avenue of the Americas, New York, NY 10020.

1 2 3 4 5 6 7 8 9 0 2QPD/2QPD 0 9 8 7 6 5 4

ISBN 0-07-286856-2

www.mhhe.com

The McGraw-Hill Companies

TABLE OF CONTENTS

Chapter 1 Quick Study 1-1 *Name* ____________

(a)	(g)
(b)	(h)
(c)	(i)
(d)	(j)
(e)	(k)
(f)	(l)

Quick Study 1-2

(a)

GAAP:

Importance:

SEC:

Importance:

FASB:

Importance:

(b)

Quick Study 1-3

(1)

(2)

(3)

Chapter 1 Quick Study 1-4 *Name* ____________________

Quick Study 1-5

Business transactions:

Business events:

Quick Study 1-6

Quick Study 1-7

(a)
(b)
(c)

Quick Study 1-8

(a)

(b)

Quick Study 1-9

Assets	=	Liabilities	+	Equity
$ 30,000		(a) ____________		$20,000
(b) ____________		$50,000		$30,000
$ 90,000		$10,000		(c) ____________

Chapter 1 Quick Study 1-10 *Name* ______________________

(a) (1) ______________________

(2) ______________________

(3) ______________________

(b)	Assets	=	Liabilities	+	Equity
		=		+	

Quick Study 1-11

(a)	______	(d)	______	(g)	______
(b)	______	(e)	______	(h)	______
(c)	______	(f)	______	(i)	______

Quick Study 1-12

Return on Assets: ______________________

____

____

Interpretation: ______________________

____

____

Chapter 1 Exercise 1-1 *Name* ______________________

(a) ______
(b) ______
(c) ______
(d) ______
(e) ______
(f) ______
(g) ______

Exercise 1-2

(1) ______
(2) ______
(3) ______
(4) ______
(5) ______
(6) ______
(7) ______

Exercise 1-3

(1) ______
(2) ______
(3) ______
(4) ______
(5) ______
(6) ______
(7) ______
(8) ______

Exercise 1-4

External User:	
External User:	
External User:	

 Exercise 1-5 **Name** ____________________

(a) ____________________

(b) ____________________

(c) ____________________

(d) ____________________

Exercise 1-6

(1) ____________________
(2) ____________________
(3) ____________________
(4) ____________________
(5) ____________________

Chapter 1 Exercise 1-7 ***Name*** ______________________

(a)

(b)

(c)

Exercise 1-8

	Assets	=	Liabilities	+	Equity
(a)					
(b)					
(c)					

Chapter 1 Exercise 1-9 *Name* ______________________

(a) ______________________

____

(b) ______________________

____

(c) ______________________

____

(d) ______________________

____

(e) ______________________

____

(f) ______________________

____

(g) ______________________

____

Exercise 1-10

(a) ______________________

____

____

(b) ______________________

____

____

(c) ______________________

____

____

(d) ______________________

____

____

(e) ______________________

____

____

Chapter 1 Exercise 1-11 *Name* ______________________

(a)

(b)

(c)

(d)

(e)

Exercise 1-12

	Cash	+	Accounts Receivable	+	Equipment	=	Accounts Payable	+	Common Stock	-	Dividends	+	Revenues	-	Expenses
(a)															
(b)															
(c)															
(d)															
(e)															
(f)															
(g)															
(h)															
(i)															
(j)															

Chapter 1 Exercise 1-13 *Name* ____________________

Exercise 1-14

Chapter 1 Exercise 1-15 *Name* ______________________

Exercise 1-16

Chapter 1 Exercise 1-17 *Name* ______________________

(1) ______________________ (5) ______________________
(2) ______________________ (6) ______________________
(3) ______________________ (7) ______________________
(4) ______________________ (8) ______________________

Exercise 1-18

Return on Assets: ______________________

____

____

____

Interpretation: ______________________

____

Exercise 1-19[B]

(a) ______________________
(b) ______________________
(c) ______________________
(d) ______________________
(e) ______________________

Chapter 1 Problem 1-1A or 1-1B *Name* ____________________

Part 1: Company______

(a)

(b)

(c)

Part 2: Company_____

(a)

(b)

(c)

 Name ______________________

Part 3: Company_____

Name ______________________________

Part 4: Company_____

Part 5: Company______

Chapter 1 Problem 1-2A or 1-2B **Name** ______________________

TRANSACTION		Balance Sheet: TOTAL ASSETS	Balance Sheet: TOTAL LIABILITIES	Balance Sheet: TOTAL EQUITY	INCOME STMT.: NET INCOME	Statement of Cash Flows: OPERATING ACTIVITIES	Statement of Cash Flows: FINANCING ACTIVITIES	Statement of Cash Flows: INVESTING ACTIVITIES
1.								
2.								
3								
4								
5								
6								
7								
8.								
9.								
10.								

 Name ____________________

Income Statement

For Year Ended December 31, 2005

Problem 1-4A or 1-4B

Balance Sheet

December 31, 2005

Problem 1-5A or 1-5B

Statement of Cash Flows

For Year Ended December 31, 2005

 Name ______________________

Statement of Retained Earnings
For Year Ended December 31, 2005

Chapter 1 Problem 1-7A or 1-7B

Parts 1 and 2

Name ____________________

	ASSETS					LIABILITIES	+	EQUITY						
DATE	CASH	+	ACCOUNTS RECEIVABLE	+	OFFICE EQUIPMENT	= ACCOUNTS PAYABLE	+	COMMON STOCK	-	DIVIDENDS	+	REVENUES	-	EXPENSES

Chapter 1 Problem 1-7A or 1-7B (Continued) *Name* ______________________

Part 3

Income Statement

Statement of Retained Earnings

Balance Sheet

Chapter 1 Problem 1-7A or 1-7B *Name* ______________________
(Continued)

Part 3

Statement of Cash Flows

Chapter 1 Problem 1-8A or 1-8B

Name ____________________

Parts 1 and 2

DATE	ASSETS					LIABILITIES	EQUITY			
	CASH +	ACCOUNTS + RECEIVABLE	OFFICE + SUPPLIES	OFFICE + EQUIPMENT	________ =	ACCOUNTS + PAYABLE	COMMON - STOCK	DIVIDENDS	+ REVENUES -	EXPENSES

Name ______________________

Part 3

Income Statement

Statement of Retained Earnings

Balance Sheet

Name ____________________

Part 3

Statement of Cash Flows

Part 4

Chapter 1 Problem 1-9A or 1-9B

Name ____________________

Parts 1 and 2

	ASSETS					LIABILITIES		EQUITY			
	CASH +	ACCOUNTS RECEIVABLE +	OFFICE SUPPLIES +	OFFICE EQUIPMENT +	BUILDING =	ACCOUNTS PAYABLE +	NOTES PAYABLE +	COMMON STOCK -	DIVIDENDS +	REVENUES -	EXPENSES
a.											
b.											
Bal.											
c.											
Bal.											
d.											
Bal.											
e.											
Bal.											
f.											
Bal.											
g.											
Bal.											
h.											
Bal.											
i.											
Bal.											
j.											
Bal.											
k.											
Bal.											

Part 3

____

____

____

Chapter 1 **Problem 1-10A or 1-10B** *Name* ______________________

(1a)

(1b)

(2)

(3)

(4)

Chapter 1 Problem 1-11A or 1-11B *Name* ______________________

(1)

(2)

(3)

(4)

Problem 1-12A or 1-12B

(1) Return:

Risk:

(2) Return:

Risk:

(3) Return:

Risk:

(4) Return:

Risk:

Chapter 1 Problem 1-13A or 1-13B *Name* ____________________

(1)	(5)
(2)	(6)
(3)	(7)
(4)	(8)

Problem 1-14A

(1) Major Activity:

(2) Major Activity:

(3) Major Activity:

Problem 1-14B

I:

A.

B.

II.

A.

B.

III.

A.

B.

Chapter 1 Serial Problem Success Systems *Name* ______________________

	ASSETS				LIABILITIES	EQUITY			
DATE	CASH +	ACCOUNTS RECEIVABLE +	COMPUTER SUPPLIES +	OFFICE EQUIPMENT =	ACCOUNTS PAYABLE +	COMMON STOCK -	DIVIDENDS +	REVENUES -	EXPENSES
Oct. 1									
3									
Bal.									
6									
Bal.									
8									
Bal.									
12									
Bal.									
15									
Bal.									
17									
Bal.									
20									
Bal.									
22									
Bal.									
28									
Bal.									
31									
Bal.									
31									
Bal.									

Chapter 1 Reporting in Action *Name* ______________________

BTN 1-1

(1)

(2)

(3)

(4)

(5) Roll On:

Chapter 1 Comparative Analysis--BTN 1-2 *Name* ____________________

Krispy Kreme	Tastykake
(1)	
(2)	
(3)	
(4)	
(5)	

Ethics Challenge--BTN 1-3

(1)

(2)

(3)

(4)

 Name ______________________

BTN 1-4

(1) ***--Request For Information--***

(2)

Chapter 1 Taking It to the Net--BTN 1-5 *Name* ______________________

1. ______________________

2. ______________________

Teamwork in Action--BTN 1-6

(1) Meeting Time and Place: ______________________

(2) Telephone and E-mail Addresses: ______________________

Instructor Notification: [ ] YES ______________________

Chapter 1 *Business Week* Activity **Name** ______________________
BTN 1-7

(1)

1
2
3
4
5
6
7
8
9
10

(2)

(3)

Entrepreneurial Decision--BTN 1-8

(1)(a)

(b)

(2)

Chapter 1 Hitting the Road **Name** ______

BTN 1-9

(1) ______

(2) ______

(3) ______

Global Decision--BTN 1-10

(1) ______

(2) ______

Chapter 2 Quick Study 2-1 *Name* ______________________

Likely source documents are:

____

____

____

____

Quick Study 2-2

(a) ______________ (f) ______________
(b) ______________ (g) ______________
(c) ______________ (h) ______________
(d) ______________ (i) ______________
(e) ______________

Quick Study 2-3

(a) ______________ (g) ______________
(b) ______________ (h) ______________
(c) ______________ (i) ______________
(d) ______________ (j) ______________
(e) ______________ (k) ______________
(f) ______________ (l) ______________

Quick Study 2-4

(a) ______________ (f) ______________
(b) ______________ (g) ______________
(c) ______________ (h) ______________
(d) ______________ (i) ______________
(e) ______________ (j) ______________

Quick Study 2-5

(a) ______________ (e) ______________
(b) ______________ (f) ______________
(c) ______________ (g) ______________
(d) ______________ (h) ______________

 Quick Study 2-6 *Name* ____________________

GENERAL JOURNAL

Date		Account Titles and Explanation	P.R.	Debit	Credit

Quick Study 2-7

____

____

____

____

____

Quick Study 2-8

(a)	(f)
(b)	(g)
(c)	(h)
(d)	(i)
(e)	(j)

Chapter 2 Exercise 2-1 *Name* ______________________

ACCOUNT	TYPE OF ACCOUNT	INCREASE (Dr. or Cr.)	NORMAL BALANCE
a.			
b.			
c.			
d.			
e.			
f.			
g.			
h.			
i.			
j.			
k.			
l.			

Exercise 2-2

Chapter 2 Exercise 2-3 *Name* ______________________

(a)

(b)

(c)

Name ______________________________

GENERAL JOURNAL

Date		Account Titles and Explanation	P.R.	Debit	Credit

 Name ______________

Cash

Photography Equipment

Common Stock

Photography Fees Earned

Office Supplies

Utilities Expense

Prepaid Insurance

Trial Balance

Chapter 2 Exercise 2-6 *Name* ______________________

Cash	

Accounts Payable	

Common Stock	

Accounts Receivable	

Dividends	

Office Supplies	

Fees Earned	

Office Equipment	

Rent Expense	

Exercise 2-7

Trial Balance

 Name ______________________

GENERAL JOURNAL

Date		Account Titles and Explanation	P.R.	Debit	Credit

Transactions not creating revenues and the reasons:

Chapter 2 Exercise 2-9 *Name* ____________________

GENERAL JOURNAL

Date		Account Titles and Explanation	P.R.	Debit	Credit

Transactions not creating revenues and the reasons:

 Exercise 2-10 Name ______________________

Income Statement

Exercise 2-11

Statement of Retained Earnings

Chapter 2 Exercise 2-12 *Name* ______________________

Balance Sheet

 Name ____________________

(a) Net Income (Loss) = [ ]
Supporting Computations:

(b) Net Income (Loss) = [ ]
Supporting Computations:

(c) Net Income (Loss) = [ ]
Supporting Computations:

(d) Net Income (Loss) = [ ]
Supporting Computations:

Chapter 2 Exercise 2-14 *Name* ______________________

	(a)	(b)	(c)	(d)

Exercise 2-15

(a) ______________________

(b) ______________________

(c) ______________________

(d) ______________________

(e) ______________________

(f) ______________________

(g) ______________________

 Name ____________________

GENERAL JOURNAL

Date		Account Titles and Explanation	P.R.	Debit	Credit
(a)					
(b)					
(c)					
(d)					
(e)					
(f)					
(g)					

 Name ______________________

	Description	(1) Difference between Debit and Credit Columns	(2) Column with the Larger Total	(3) Identify account(s) incorrectly stated	(4) Amount that account(s) is overstated or understated
(a)	$2,400 debit to Rent Expense is posted as a $1,590 debit.	$810	Credit	Rent Expense	Rent Expense is understated by $810
(b)					
(c)					
(d)					
(e)					
(f)					
(g)					

 Name ______________________

(a) ______________________

____

____

____

(b) ______________________

____

____

____

(c) ______________________

____

____

____

(d) ______________________

____

____

____

(e) ______________________

____

____

____

Chapter 2 Exercise 2-19 *Name* ______________________

Part a

(1) ______________________

(2) ______________________

(3) ______________________

(4) ______________________

(5) ______________________

(6) ______________________

Part b

Part c

Part d

Part e

Part f

Chapter 2 Problem 2-1A or 2-1B *Name* ______________________

Part 1

GENERAL JOURNAL

Date		Account Titles and Explanation	P.R.	Debit	Credit

Date		Account Titles and Explanation	P.R.	Debit	Credit

 Name ______________________

Part 2

GENERAL LEDGER

Cash — ACCOUNT NO. 101

Date	Explanation	P.R.	DEBIT	CREDIT	BALANCE

Accounts Receivable — ACCOUNT NO. 106

Date	Explanation	P.R.	DEBIT	CREDIT	BALANCE

Office Supplies — ACCOUNT NO. 124

Date	Explanation	P.R.	DEBIT	CREDIT	BALANCE

Prepaid Insurance — ACCOUNT NO. 128

Date	Explanation	P.R.	DEBIT	CREDIT	BALANCE

Chapter 2 Problem 2-1A or 2-1B *Name* ____________________
Part 2 (Continued)

Prepaid Rent ACCOUNT NO. 131

Date	Explanation	P.R.	DEBIT	CREDIT	BALANCE

Office Equipment ACCOUNT NO. 163

Date	Explanation	P.R.	DEBIT	CREDIT	BALANCE

Accounts Payable ACCOUNT NO. 201

Date	Explanation	P.R.	DEBIT	CREDIT	BALANCE

Common Stock ACCOUNT NO. 307

Date	Explanation	P.R.	DEBIT	CREDIT	BALANCE

Dividends ACCOUNT NO. 319

Date	Explanation	P.R.	DEBIT	CREDIT	BALANCE

Chapter 2 Problem 2-1A or 2-1B *Name* ______________________

Part 2 (Continued)

Service Fees Earned** ACCOUNT NO. 401

Date	Explanation	P.R.	DEBIT	CREDIT	BALANCE

Services Revenue* ACCOUNT NO. 403

Date	Explanation	P.R.	DEBIT	CREDIT	BALANCE

Utilities Expense ACCOUNT NO. 690

Date	Explanation	P.R.	DEBIT	CREDIT	BALANCE

* Problem 2-1A only.

** Problem 2-1B only

Name ______________________________

Trial Balance

Chapter 2 Problem 2-2A or 2-2B *Name* ____________________

Part 1

GENERAL JOURNAL

Date		Account Titles and Explanation	P.R.	Debit	Credit

Name ______________________

GENERAL JOURNAL

Date		Account Titles and Explanation	P.R.	Debit	Credit

 Name ____________________

Part 2

Cash No. 101

DATE	PR	Debit	Credit	Balance

Accounts Payable No. 201

DATE	PR	Debit	Credit	Balance

Notes Payable No. 250

DATE	PR	Debit	Credit	Balance

Common Stock No. 307

DATE	PR	Debit	Credit	Balance

Accounts Receivable No. 106

DATE	PR	Debit	Credit	Balance

Dividends No. 319

DATE	PR	Debit	Credit	Balance

__________Fees Earned No. 402

DATE	PR	Debit	Credit	Balance

Prepaid Insurance No. 108

DATE	PR	Debit	Credit	Balance

Office Equipment No. 163

DATE	PR	Debit	Credit	Balance

Wages Expense No. 601

DATE	PR	Debit	Credit	Balance

__________Equipment No. 164

DATE	PR	Debit	Credit	Balance

__________Rental Expense No. 602

DATE	PR	Debit	Credit	Balance

Building No. 170

DATE	PR	Debit	Credit	Balance

Advertising Expense No. 603

DATE	PR	Debit	Credit	Balance

Land No. 172

DATE	PR	Debit	Credit	Balance

Repairs Expense No. 604

DATE	PR	Debit	Credit	Balance

 Name ______________________

Part 3

Trial Balance

Chapter 2 Problem 2-3A or 2-3B *Name* ______________________

Part 1

GENERAL JOURNAL

Date		Account Titles and Explanation	P.R.	Debit	Credit

Chapter 2 Problem 2-3A or 2-3B *Name* ______________________

Part 1 (Continued)

Date		Account Titles and Explanation	P.R.	Debit	Credit

Chapter 2 Problem 2-3A or 2-3B *Name* ______________________

Part 2

GENERAL LEDGER

Cash ACCOUNT NO. 101

Date	Explanation	P.R.	DEBIT	CREDIT	BALANCE

Accounts Receivable ACCOUNT NO. 106

Date	Explanation	P.R.	DEBIT	CREDIT	BALANCE

Office Supplies ACCOUNT NO. 124

Date	Explanation	P.R.	DEBIT	CREDIT	BALANCE

Prepaid Insurance ACCOUNT NO. 128

Date	Explanation	P.R.	DEBIT	CREDIT	BALANCE

Chapter 2 Problem 2-3A or 2-3B *Name* ____________________
Part 2 (Continued)

Prepaid Rent ACCOUNT NO. 131

Date	Explanation	P.R.	DEBIT	CREDIT	BALANCE

Office Equipment ACCOUNT NO. 163

Date	Explanation	P.R.	DEBIT	CREDIT	BALANCE

Accounts Payable ACCOUNT NO. 201

Date	Explanation	P.R.	DEBIT	CREDIT	BALANCE

Common Stock ACCOUNT NO. 307

Date	Explanation	P.R.	DEBIT	CREDIT	BALANCE

Dividends ACCOUNT NO. 319

Date	Explanation	P.R.	DEBIT	CREDIT	BALANCE

Chapter 2 Problem 2-3A or 2-3B *Name* ______________________

Part 2 (Continued)

Services Revenue ACCOUNT NO. 403

Date	Explanation	P.R.	DEBIT	CREDIT	BALANCE

Utilities Expense ACCOUNT NO. 690

Date	Explanation	P.R.	DEBIT	CREDIT	BALANCE

Part 3

Trial Balance

Chapter 2 Problem 2-4A or 2-4B *Name* ______________________

Part 1

Balance Sheet

Balance Sheet

 Name ______________________

Part 2

Net Income Computation:

Part 3

Debt Ratio:

Chapter 2 Problem 2-5A or 2-5B *Name* ______________________

Part 1

Trial Balance

Part 2

Seven Most Likely Transactions (following order of trial balance):

(1)

(2)

(3)

(4)

(5)

(6)

(7)

Report of Cash Received and Cash Paid

Chapter 2 Problem 2-6A or 2-6B *Name* ____________________

Part 1

GENERAL JOURNAL

Date		Account Titles and Explanation	P.R.	Debit	Credit

Chapter 2 Problem 2-6A or 2-6B ***Name*** ______________________________

Part 1 (Continued)

Date		Account Titles and Explanation	P.R.	Debit	Credit

Chapter 2 Problem 2-6A or 2-6B *Name* ____________________

Part 2

Cash No. 101

DATE	PR	Debit	Credit	Balance

Land No. 172

DATE	PR	Debit	Credit	Balance

Accounts Payable No. 201

DATE	PR	Debit	Credit	Balance

Notes Payable No. 250

DATE	PR	Debit	Credit	Balance

Accounts Receivable No. 106

DATE	PR	Debit	Credit	Balance

Common Stock No. 307

DATE	PR	Debit	Credit	Balance

Office Supplies No. 108

DATE	PR	Debit	Credit	Balance

Dividends No. 319

DATE	PR	Debit	Credit	Balance

Office Equipment No. 163

DATE	PR	Debit	Credit	Balance

Fees Earned No. 402

DATE	PR	Debit	Credit	Balance

Automobiles No. 164

DATE	PR	Debit	Credit	Balance

Salaries Expense No. 601

DATE	PR	Debit	Credit	Balance

Building No. 170

DATE	PR	Debit	Credit	Balance

Utilities Expense No. 602

DATE	PR	Debit	Credit	Balance

Chapter 2 Problem 2-6A or 2-6B *Name* ____________________

Part 3

Trial Balance

Chapter 2 Serial Problem *Name* ____________________

Part 1 Success Systems

GENERAL JOURNAL

Date		Account Titles and Explanation	P.R.	Debit	Credit

Name ______________________

Date		Account Titles and Explanation	P.R.	Debit	Credit

Date		Account Titles and Explanation	P.R.	Debit	Credit

Chapter 2 Serial Problem
Part 2 (Continued)

Name ______________________

GENERAL LEDGER

Cash — ACCOUNT NO. 101

Date	Explanation	P.R.	DEBIT	CREDIT	BALANCE

Accounts Receivable — ACCOUNT NO. 106

Date	Explanation	P.R.	DEBIT	CREDIT	BALANCE

Name ______________________

Computer Supplies ACCOUNT NO. 126

Date	Explanation	P.R.	DEBIT	CREDIT	BALANCE

Prepaid Insurance ACCOUNT NO. 128

Date	Explanation	P.R.	DEBIT	CREDIT	BALANCE

Prepaid Rent ACCOUNT NO. 131

Date	Explanation	P.R.	DEBIT	CREDIT	BALANCE

Office Equipment ACCOUNT NO. 163

Date	Explanation	P.R.	DEBIT	CREDIT	BALANCE

Computer Equipment ACCOUNT NO. 167

Date	Explanation	P.R.	DEBIT	CREDIT	BALANCE

Chapter 2 Serial Problem *Name* ____________________
Part 2 (Continued)

Accounts Payable **ACCOUNT NO. 201**

Date	Explanation	P.R.	DEBIT	CREDIT	BALANCE

Common Stock **ACCOUNT NO. 307**

Date	Explanation	P.R.	DEBIT	CREDIT	BALANCE

Dividends **ACCOUNT NO. 319**

Date	Explanation	P.R.	DEBIT	CREDIT	BALANCE

Computer Services Revenue **ACCOUNT NO. 403**

Date	Explanation	P.R.	DEBIT	CREDIT	BALANCE

Chapter 2 Serial Problem Name ____________________
Part 2 (Continued)

Wages Expense ACCOUNT NO. 623

Date	Explanation	P.R.	DEBIT	CREDIT	BALANCE

Advertising Expense ACCOUNT NO. 655

Date	Explanation	P.R.	DEBIT	CREDIT	BALANCE

Mileage Expense ACCOUNT NO. 676

Date	Explanation	P.R.	DEBIT	CREDIT	BALANCE

Miscellaneous Expense ACCOUNT NO. 677

Date	Explanation	P.R.	DEBIT	CREDIT	BALANCE

Repairs Expense-Computer ACCOUNT NO. 684

Date	Explanation	P.R.	DEBIT	CREDIT	BALANCE

Name ______________________

Trial Balance

Chapter 2 Reporting in Action *Name* ______________________

BTN 2-1

(1)

(2)

(3)

(4)

(5) Roll On:

Comparative Analysis--BTN 2-2

(1) Current Year Debt Ratio

Prior Year Debt Ratio

(2) Current Year Debt Ratio

Prior Year Debt Ratio

(3)

Chapter 2 Ethics Challenge--BTN 2-3 *Name* ____________________

Name ______________________

MEMORANDUM

TO:

FROM:

SUBJECT:

DATE:

 Name ______________________

(1) ______________________

(2) ______________________

(3) ______________________

Chapter 2 Teamwork in Action ***Name*** ____________________

BTN 2-6

(1) Component selected:

(2) (a)

(b)

(c)

(d)

(e)

(3) Presentation Notes:

***Business Week* Activity--BTN 2-7**

(1)

(2)

(3)

Chapter 2 Entrepreneurial Decision *Name* ______________________

BTN 2-8

(1)

Balance Sheet

(2)

(3)

Chapter 2 Entrepreneurial Decision *Name* ____________________

BTN 2-9

(1) ____________________

(2) ____________________

 Name ______________________

BTN 2-10

(1) ______________________

(2) ______________________

(3) ______________________

(4) ______________________

Name ______________________

(1) ______________________

(2) ______________________

(3) ______________________

Chapter 3 Quick Study 3-1 *Name* ______________________

(a) ______________________

(b) ______________________

(c) ______________________

(d) ______________________

(e) ______________________

Quick Study 3-2

GENERAL JOURNAL

Date		Account Titles and Explanation	P.R	Debit	Credit
(a)					
(b)					

Quick Study 3-3

GENERAL JOURNAL

Date		Account Titles and Explanation	P.R	Debit	Credit
(a)					

(b) ______________________

 Quick Study 3-4 *Name* ______________________

GENERAL JOURNAL

Date		Account Titles and Explanation	P.R	Debit	Credit
(a)					
(b)					

Quick Study 3-5

GENERAL JOURNAL

Date		Account Titles and Explanation	P.R	Debit	Credit

Quick Study 3-6

	Dr./Cr.	Account Titles	Financial Statement
(a)	Debit		
	Credit		
(b)	Debit		
	Credit		
(c)	Debit		
	Credit		
(d)	Debit		
	Credit		
(e)	Debit		
	Credit		

 Quick Study 3-7 *Name* ______________________

	Debit	Credit
(1)		
(2)		
(3)		

Quick Study 3-8

Answer is ________
Supporting work:

Quick Study 3-9

Cash Basis:

Accrual Basis

Quick Study 3-10

Answer is ________
Supporting work:

 Quick Study 3-11 *Name* ______________________

____
____
____
____
____
____
____
____
____
____

Quick Study 3-12

Steps

1st ______________________
2nd ______________________
3rd ______________________
4th ______________________
5th ______________________
6th ______________________
7th ______________________
8th ______________________
9th ______________________

Quick Study 3-13

(1) ______________________ (5) ______________________
(2) ______________________ (6) ______________________
(3) ______________________ (7) ______________________
(4) ______________________ (8) ______________________

GENERAL JOURNAL

Date		Account Titles and Explanation	P. R.	Debit	Credit

Quick Study 3-15

Chapter 3 Quick Study 3-16 *Name* ____________________

Profit Margin:

Interpretation of Profit Margin:

Quick Study 3-17

Quick Study 3-18[A]

Answer is ____________

Supporting work:

Quick Study 3-19[B]

(a) (d)

(b) (e)

(c) (f)

 Quick Study 3-20[B] *Name* ____________________

Terrel Company										
Worksheet										
ACCOUNT TITLE	Unadjusted Trial Balance		Adjustments		Adjusted Trial Balance		Income Statement		Balance Sheet	
	Dr.	Cr.	Dr.	Cr.	Dr.	Cr.	Dr.	Cr.	Dr.	Cr.
Prepaid rent										
Service revenue										
Wages expense										
Accounts receivable										
Wages payable										
Rent expense										

Quick Study 3-21[C]

GENERAL JOURNAL

Date	Account Titles and Explanation	P. R.	Debit	Credit

 Name ______________________

GENERAL JOURNAL

Date		Account Titles and Explanation	P.R	Debit	Credit
(a)					
(b)					
(c)					
(d)					
(e)					
(f)					
(g)					

Notes:

 Name ____________________

GENERAL JOURNAL

Date		Account Titles and Explanation	P.R	Debit	Credit
(a)					
(b)					
(c)					
(d)					
(e)					
(f)					

Notes:

Chapter 3 Exercise 3-3 *Name* ____________________

GENERAL JOURNAL

Date		Account Titles and Explanation	P.R	Debit	Credit
Adjusting Entry:					
Payday Entry:					

Chapter 3 Exercise 3-4 *Name* ____________

(a)

GENERAL JOURNAL

Date		Account Titles and Explanation	P.R.	Debit	Credit
Adjusting Entry:					
Journal Entry (Next Period):					

(b)

GENERAL JOURNAL

Date		Account Titles and Explanation	P.R	Debit	Credit
Adjusting Entry:					
Journal Entry (Next Period):					

(c)

GENERAL JOURNAL

Date		Account Titles and Explanation	P.R.	Debit	Credit
Adjusting Entry:					
Journal Entry (Next Period):					

Exercise 3-5

Balance Sheet Insurance Asset Using:		
Date of:	***Accrual Basis***	***Cash Basis***
12/31/2003		
12/31/2004		
12/31/2005		
12/31/2006		

Insurance Expense Using:		
Year	***Accrual Basis***	***Cash Basis***
2003		
2004		
2005		
2006		
Total		

Supporting work:

Chapter 3 Exercise 3-6 *Name* ______________________

1. Closing

GENERAL JOURNAL

Date		Account Titles and Explanation	P. R.	Debit	Credit

2. Post-closing Trial Balance

Post-Closing Trial Balance

Balance Sheet

 Name ________________

Income Statement

Statement of Retained Earnings

Chapter 3 Exercise 3-9 *Name* ______________________

Profit Margin Calculation:

(a)

(b)

(c)

(d)

(e)

Most Profitable:

Interpretation of Profit Margin:

Exercise 3-10

Current Ratio:

Interpretation:

 Name ______________________

	Current Assets	Current Liabilities	Current Ratio
Case 1			
Case 2			
Case 3			
Case 4			
Case 5			

Analysis: ______________________

Chapter 3 Exercise 3-12[A] *Name* ____________________

GENERAL JOURNAL

Date		Account Titles and Explanation	P.R.	Debit	Credit
(a)					
(b)					
(c)					
(d)					
(e)					
(f)					
(g)					

Chapter 3 Exercise 3-13[A] Name ____________________

GENERAL JOURNAL

Date		Account Titles and Explanation	P.R.	Debit	Credit
(a)					
(b)					

Chapter 3 Exercise 3-13[A] *Name* ______________________________
(Continued)

(c)
Method in Part (a):
Unearned Fees = $ ________________

Fees Earned = $ ________________

Method in Part (b):
Unearned Fees = $ ________________

Fees Earned = $ ________________

Chapter 3 **Exercise 3-14B** ***Name*** ______________________

Dalton Delivery Company
Work Sheet
For Year Ended December 31, 2005

ACCOUNT TITLE	Unadjusted Trial Balance		Adjustments		Adjusted Trial Balance		Income Statement		Balance Sheet	
	Dr.	Cr.	Dr.	Cr.	Dr.	Cr.	Dr.	Cr.	Dr.	Cr.

2. Closing Entries

GENERAL JOURNAL

Date		Account Titles and Explanation	P. R.	Debit	Credit

On the Balance Sheet:

Chapter 3 Exercise 3-15[C] *Name* ______________________________

Part 1

GENERAL JOURNAL

Date		Account Titles and Explanation	P. R.	Debit	Credit

Part 2

GENERAL JOURNAL

Date		Account Titles and Explanation	P. R.	Debit	Credit

Part 3

GENERAL JOURNAL

Date		Account Titles and Explanation	P. R.	Debit	Credit

 Name ______________________________

GENERAL JOURNAL

Date		Account Titles and Explanation	P. R.	Debit	Credit

Chapter 3 Problem 3-1A or 3-1B *Name* ______________________________

Part 1

GENERAL JOURNAL

Date		Account Titles and Explanation	P.R.	Debit	Credit

Chapter 3 Problem 3-1A or 3-1B *Name* ____________________
Part 2 (Continued)

GENERAL JOURNAL

Date		Account Titles and Explanation	P.R.	Debit	Credit

Chapter 3 Problem 3-2A or 3-2B Name ______________

Parts 1 & 2

Cash

Accounts Receivable

Teaching Supplies

Prepaid Insurance

Prepaid Rent

Professional Library

Accumulated Depreciation --- Professional Library

Equipment

Accumulated Depreciation-- Equipment

Accounts Payable

Salaries Payable

Unearned Training Fees

Common Stock

Retained Earnings

Dividends

Chapter 3 Problem 3-2A or 3-2B
Parts 1 & 2 (Continued)

Name ______________________

Tuition Fees Earned	

Rent Expense	

Training Fees Earned	

Teaching Supplies Expense	

Depreciation Expense--Professional Library	

Advertising Expense	

Depreciation Expense--Equipment	

Utilities Expense	

Salaries Expense	

Insurance Expense	

Chapter 3 Problem 3-2A or 3-2B *Name* ____________________

Part 2 (Continued)

GENERAL JOURNAL

Date		Account Titles and Explanation	P.R.	Debit	Credit

Chapter 3 Problem 3-2A or 3-2B *Name* ____________
Part 3 (Continued)

Adjusted Trial Balance

Name ______________________

Income Statement

Statement of Retained Earnings

Name ______________________

Balance Sheet

Chapter 3 Problem 3-3A or 3-3B *Name* ______________________

Part 1

Income Statement

Statement of Retained Earnings

Balance Sheet

 Name ______________________

Work Sheet

____

NO.	ACCOUNT TITLES	ADJUSTED TRIAL BALANCE		AMOUNTS FOR CLOSING ENTRIES		POST-CLOSING TRIAL BALANCE	
		DR	CR	DR	CR	DR	CR

Chapter 3 Problem 3-3A or 3-3B *Name* ______________________
Parts 2 & 3 (Continued)
Closing Entries

GENERAL JOURNAL

Date		Account Titles and Explanation	P. R.	Debit	Credit

Part 4

Financial Statement Changes:

Chapter 3 **Problem 3-4A or 3-4B** *Name* ____________________

Part 1

GENERAL JOURNAL

Cash **ACCOUNT NO. 101**

DATE	EXPLANATION	P.R.	DEBIT	CREDIT	BALANCE

Accounts Receivable **ACCOUNT NO. 106**

DATE	EXPLANATION	P.R.	DEBIT	CREDIT	BALANCE

Office Supplies **ACCOUNT NO. 124**

DATE	EXPLANATION	P.R.	DEBIT	CREDIT	BALANCE

Prepaid Insurance **ACCOUNT NO. 128**

DATE	EXPLANATION	P.R.	DEBIT	CREDIT	BALANCE

Name ______________________

Computer Equipment*

ACCOUNT NO. 167

DATE	EXPLANATION	P.R.	DEBIT	CREDIT	BALANCE

Accumulated Depreciation-Computer Equipment*

ACCOUNT NO. 168

DATE	EXPLANATION	P.R.	DEBIT	CREDIT	BALANCE

Building**

ACCOUNT NO. 173

DATE	EXPLANATION	P.R.	DEBIT	CREDIT	BALANCE

Accumulated Depreciation-Buildings**

ACCOUNT NO. 174

DATE	EXPLANATION	P.R.	DEBIT	CREDIT	BALANCE

Salaries Payable

ACCOUNT NO. 209

DATE	EXPLANATION	P.R.	DEBIT	CREDIT	BALANCE

Common Stock

ACCOUNT NO. 307

DATE	EXPLANATION	P.R.	DEBIT	CREDIT	BALANCE

Retained Earnings

ACCOUNT NO. 318

DATE	EXPLANATION	P.R.	DEBIT	CREDIT	BALANCE

* Problem 3-4A only.

** Problem 3-4B only.

Name ____________________

Dividends — ACCOUNT NO. 319

DATE	EXPLANATION	P.R.	DEBIT	CREDIT	BALANCE

Storage Fees Earned** — ACCOUNT NO. 401

DATE	EXPLANATION	P.R.	DEBIT	CREDIT	BALANCE

Commissions Earned* — ACCOUNT NO. 405

DATE	EXPLANATION	P.R.	DEBIT	CREDIT	BALANCE

Depreciation Expense--Buildings** — ACCOUNT NO. 606

DATE	EXPLANATION	P.R.	DEBIT	CREDIT	BALANCE

Depreciation Expense-Computer Equipment* — ACCOUNT NO. 612

DATE	EXPLANATION	P.R.	DEBIT	CREDIT	BALANCE

* Problem 3-4A only.

** Problem 3-4B only.

Name ______________________

Salaries Expense ACCOUNT NO. 622

DATE	EXPLANATION	P.R.	DEBIT	CREDIT	BALANCE

Insurance Expense ACCOUNT NO. 637

DATE	EXPLANATION	P.R.	DEBIT	CREDIT	BALANCE

Rent Expense ACCOUNT NO. 640

DATE	EXPLANATION	P.R.	DEBIT	CREDIT	BALANCE

Office Supplies Expense ACCOUNT NO. 650

DATE	EXPLANATION	P.R.	DEBIT	CREDIT	BALANCE

Repairs Expense ACCOUNT NO. 684

DATE	EXPLANATION	P.R.	DEBIT	CREDIT	BALANCE

Telephone Expense ACCOUNT NO. 688

DATE	EXPLANATION	P.R.	DEBIT	CREDIT	BALANCE

Chapter 3 Problem 3-4A or 3-4B *Name* ______________________
Part 1 (Continued)

Income Summary ACCOUNT NO. 901

DATE	EXPLANATION	P.R.	DEBIT	CREDIT	BALANCE

Chapter 3 Problem 3-4A or 3-4B Name

Part 2

GENERAL JOURNAL

Date		Account Titles and Explanation	P. R.	Debit	Credit

 Name ____________________

Part 3

Unadjusted Trial Balance

Name ____________________

GENERAL JOURNAL

Date		Account Titles and Explanation	P. R.	Debit	Credit

Income Statement

Statement of Retained Earnings

Balance Sheet

Chapter 3 Problem 3-4A or 3-4B *Name* ______________________

Part 6 (Continued)

Closing Entries:

GENERAL JOURNAL

Date		Account Titles and Explanation	P. R.	Debit	Credit

Part 7

Post-Closing Trial Balance

Chapter 3 Problem 3-5A or 3-5B *Name* ______________________

(1)	(6)	(11)	(16)
(2)	(7)	(12)	(17)
(3)	(8)	(13)	(18)
(4)	(9)	(14)	(19)
(5)	(10)	(15)	(20)

Chapter 3 Problem 3-6A or 3-6B *Name* ____________________

Part 1

GENERAL JOURNAL

Date		Account Titles and Explanation	P.R.	Debit	Credit

Name ______________________

GENERAL JOURNAL

Date		Account Titles and Explanation	P.R.	Debit	Credit

Chapter 3 Problem 3-7A or 3-7B

Part 1

Name ____________________

Work Sheet

No.	Account Title	Unadjusted Trial Balance		Adjustments		Adjusted Trial Balance		Income Statement		Balance Sheet	
		Dr.	Cr.	Dr.	Cr.	Dr.	Cr.	Dr.	Cr.	Dr.	Cr.

Chapter 3 Problem 3-7A or 3-7B *Name* ______________________

Part 2 (Continued)

Adjusting Entries

GENERAL JOURNAL

Date		Account Titles and Explanation	P. R.	Debit	Credit

Chapter 3 Problem 3-7A or 3-7B *Name* ______________________
Part 2 (Continued)
Closing Entries

GENERAL JOURNAL

Date		Account Titles and Explanation	P. R.	Debit	Credit

Income Statement

Statement of Retained Earnings

Balance Sheet

Chapter 3 Problem 3-7A or 3-7B *Name* ____________________

Part 4 (Continued)

(a)

(b)

Chapter 3 Serial Problem *Name* ______________________

Part 1 Success Systems

Journal Entries

GENERAL JOURNAL

Date		Account Titles and Explanation	P.R.	Debit	Credit

Chapter 3 Serial Problem Name ______________________

Part 2 Success Systems

Adjusting Entries

GENERAL JOURNAL

Date		Account Titles and Explanation	P.R.	Debit	Credit

Chapter 3 Serial Problem Name ______________________
Part 1 & 2 Success Systems
(Continued)

GENERAL LEDGER

Cash ACCOUNT NO. 101

Date	Explanation	P.R.	DEBIT	CREDIT	BALANCE
2004 Nov. 30	Balance				48,052

Accounts Receivable ACCOUNT NO. 106

Date	Explanation	P.R.	DEBIT	CREDIT	BALANCE
2004 Nov. 30	Balance				12,618

Computer Supplies ACCOUNT NO. 126

Date	Explanation	P.R.	DEBIT	CREDIT	BALANCE
2004 Nov. 30	Balance				2,545

Chapter 3 Serial Problem
Parts 1 & 2 Success Systems
(Continued)

Name ______________________

Prepaid Insurance — ACCOUNT NO. 128

Date	Explanation	P.R.	DEBIT	CREDIT	BALANCE
2004 Nov. 30	Balance				2,220

Prepaid Rent — ACCOUNT NO. 131

Date	Explanation	P.R.	DEBIT	CREDIT	BALANCE
2004 Nov. 30	Balance				3,300

Office Equipment — ACCOUNT NO. 163

Date	Explanation	P.R.	DEBIT	CREDIT	BALANCE
2004 Nov. 30	Balance				8,000

Accumulated Depreciation--Office Equipment — ACCOUNT NO. 164

Date	Explanation	P.R.	DEBIT	CREDIT	BALANCE

Computer Equipment — ACCOUNT NO. 167

Date	Explanation	P.R.	DEBIT	CREDIT	BALANCE
2004 Nov. 30	Balance				20,000

Chapter 3 Serial Problem
Parts 1 & 2 Success Systems
(Continued)

Name ______________________

Accumulated Depreciation--Computer Equipment ACCOUNT NO. 168

Date	Explanation	P.R.	DEBIT	CREDIT	BALANCE

Accounts Payable ACCOUNT NO. 201

Date	Explanation	P.R.	DEBIT	CREDIT	BALANCE
2004 Nov. 30	Balance				0

Wages Payable ACCOUNT NO. 210

Date	Explanation	P.R.	DEBIT	CREDIT	BALANCE

Unearned Computer Services Revenue ACCOUNT NO. 236

Date	Explanation	P.R.	DEBIT	CREDIT	BALANCE

Common Stock ACCOUNT NO. 307

Date	Explanation	P.R.	DEBIT	CREDIT	BALANCE
2004 Nov. 30	Balance				83,000

Retained Earnings ACCOUNT NO. 318

Date	Explanation	P.R.	DEBIT	CREDIT	BALANCE
2004 Nov. 30	Balance				0

Name ______________________

Dividends ACCOUNT NO. 319

Date	Explanation	P.R.	DEBIT	CREDIT	BALANCE
2004 Nov. 30	Balance				5,600

Computer Services Revenue ACCOUNT NO. 403

Date	Explanation	P.R.	DEBIT	CREDIT	BALANCE
2004 Nov. 30	Balance				25,659

Depreciation Expense--Office Equipment ACCOUNT NO. 612

Date	Explanation	P.R.	DEBIT	CREDIT	BALANCE

Depreciation Expense--Computer Equipment ACCOUNT NO. 613

Date	Explanation	P.R.	DEBIT	CREDIT	BALANCE

Wages Expense ACCOUNT NO. 623

Date	Explanation	P.R.	DEBIT	CREDIT	BALANCE
2004 Nov. 30	Balance				2,625

Name ____________________

Insurance Expense ACCOUNT NO. 637

Date	Explanation	P.R.	DEBIT	CREDIT	BALANCE

Rent Expense ACCOUNT NO. 640

Date	Explanation	P.R.	DEBIT	CREDIT	BALANCE

Computer Supplies Expense ACCOUNT NO. 652

Date	Explanation	P.R.	DEBIT	CREDIT	BALANCE

Advertising Expense ACCOUNT NO. 655

Date	Explanation	P.R.	DEBIT	CREDIT	BALANCE
2004 Nov. 30	Balance				1,940

Mileage Expense ACCOUNT NO. 676

Date	Explanation	P.R.	DEBIT	CREDIT	BALANCE
2004 Nov. 30	Balance				704

Chapter 3 Serial Problem
Parts 1 & 2 Success Systems
(Continued)

Name ______________________________

Miscellaneous Expense ACCOUNT NO. 677

Date	Explanation	P.R.	DEBIT	CREDIT	BALANCE
2004 Nov. 30	Balance				250

Repairs Expense--Computer ACCOUNT NO. 684

Date	Explanation	P.R.	DEBIT	CREDIT	BALANCE
2004 Nov. 30	Balance				805

Income Summary ACCOUNT NO. 901

Date	Explanation	P.R.	DEBIT	CREDIT	BALANCE

Chapter 3 Serial Problem **Name** ____________________

Part 3 Success Systems (Continued)

SUCCESS SYSTEMS
Adjusted Trial Balance
December 31, 2004

Name ________________________

SUCCESS SYSTEMS
Income Statement
For Three Months Ended December 31, 2004

SUCCESS SYSTEMS
Statement of Retained Earnings
For Three Months Ended December 31, 2004

Name ______________________

SUCCESS SYSTEMS
Balance Sheet
December 31, 2004

Chapter 3 **Serial Problem** *Name* ______________________________

Part 5 **Success Systems**

Closing Entries

GENERAL JOURNAL

Date		Account Titles and Explanation	P. R.	Debit	Credit

Chapter 3 Serial Problem **Name** ____________________

Part 6 Success Systems (Continued)

SUCCESS SYSTEMS
Post-Closing Trial Balance
December 31, 2004

Chapter 3 Reporting in Action--BTN 3-1 *Name* ____________________

(1)

(2)

(3) 2003 Profit Margin:

2002 Profit Margin:

(4)

(5)

(6)

(7) Roll On:

Chapter 3 Comparative Analysis--BTN 3-2 *Name* ______________________

(1) Krispy Kreme

Current Year Profit Margin:

Prior Year Profit Margin:

Tastykake

Current Year Profit Margin:

Prior Year Profit Margin:

(2) Analysis

(3)

(4)

(5)

(6)

Chapter 3 Ethics Challenge--BTN 3-3 ***Name*** ______________________________

(1)

(2)

 Name ______________________________

MEMORANDUM

TO:
FROM:
SUBJECT:
DATE:

 Name ______________________

(1) ______________________

(2) ______________________

(3) ______________________

(4) ______________________

(5) ______________________

(6) ______________________

(7) ______________________

 Name ______________________

(1) ______________________

(2) ______________________

(3) ______________________

Chapter 3 Teamwork in Action--BTN 3-7 *Name* ______________________

Chapter 3 *Business Week Activity* **Name** ______________________

BTN 3-8

(1) ______________________

(2) ______________________

(3) ______________________

(4) ______________________

Chapter 3 **Business Week Activity** *Name* ______________________

BTN 3-9

(1)

(2)

(3)

(4)

Hitting the Road--BTN 3-10

1.

2.

3.

4.

5.

Chapter 3 Entrepreneurial Decision *Name* ______________________

BTN 3-11

(1) ______________________

(2) ______________________

(3) ______________________

(4) ______________________

Chapter 3 Global Decision *Name* ______________________

BTN 3-12

(1)

(2)

(3) 2002 Profit Margin:

2001 Profit Margin:

(4)

(5)

 Name ____________________

GENERAL JOURNAL

Date		Account Titles and Explanation	P. R.	Debit	Credit

 Name ______________________

GENERAL JOURNAL

Date		Account Titles and Explanation	P. R.	Debit	Credit

 Name ____________________

Case (a)

Case (b)

Case (c)

Case (d)

Interpretation of (a)

Quick Study 4-4

GENERAL JOURNAL

Date		Account Titles and Explanation	P. R.	Debit	Credit

 Name ________________

GENERAL JOURNAL

Date		Account Titles and Explanation	P. R.	Debit	Credit

Quick Study 4-6:

Acid-Test Ratio:

Interpretation:

Quick Study 4-7

Name ____________________

Quick Study 4-8

(a)
(b)
(c)
(d)

 Quick Study 4-9 *Name* ______________________

GENERAL JOURNAL

Date		Account Titles and Explanation	P. R.	Debit	Credit

Quick Study 4-10

GENERAL JOURNAL

Date		Account Titles and Explanation	P. R.	Debit	Credit

 Name ______________________

GENERAL JOURNAL

Date		Account Titles and Explanation	P. R.	Debit	Credit

Chapter 4 Exercise 4-2 *Name* ______________________________

(1) BUYER

GENERAL JOURNAL

Date		Account Titles and Explanation	P. R.	Debit	Credit

(2) SELLER

GENERAL JOURNAL

Date		Account Titles and Explanation	P. R.	Debit	Credit

(3)

____

____

____

____

____

____

____

____

____

____

____

____

Exercise 4-3

(1)	(6)
(2)	(7)
(3)	(8)
(4)	(9)
(5)	(10)

 Name ______________________

GENERAL JOURNAL

Date	Account Titles and Explanation	P. R.	Debit	Credit
Entries for Sale of Merchandise:				
Entries for (a):				
Entries for (b):				
Entries for (c):				

 Name ______________________________

GENERAL JOURNAL

Date		Account Titles and Explanation	P. R.	Debit	Credit
Entries for Purchase of Merchandise:					
Entries for (a):					
Entries for (b):					
Entries for (c):					

Chapter 4 Exercise 4-6 *Name* ____________________

(1) BUYER

GENERAL JOURNAL

Date		Account Titles and Explanation	P. R.	Debit	Credit

(1) SELLER

GENERAL JOURNAL

Date		Account Titles and Explanation	P. R.	Debit	Credit

Name ______________________________

 Name ____________________

Merchandise Inventory	

Cost of Goods Sold	

Chapter 4 Exercise 4-9 *Name* ______________________

	(a)	(b)	(c)	(d)	(e)
Sales	$ 60,000	$ 42,500	$ 36,000		$ 23,600
Cost of goods sold					
Merchandise inventory (beg.)	6,000	17,050	7,500	7,000	2,560
Total cost of merch. purchases	36,000			32,000	5,600
Merchandise inventory (ending)		(2,700)	(9,000)	(6,600)	
Cost of goods sold	34,050	15,900			5,600
Gross profit			3,750	45,600	
Expenses	9,000	10,650	12,150	2,600	6,000
Net income (loss)		$ 15,950	$ (8,400)	$ 43,000	

Work space:

Exercise 4-10

Adjusting Entries:

GENERAL JOURNAL

Date		Account Titles and Explanation	P. R.	Debit	Credit

Chapter 4 Exercise 4-10 *Name* ______________________________

Closing Entries:

GENERAL JOURNAL

Date		Account Titles and Explanation	P. R.	Debit	Credit

 Name ______________________________

	Case X	Case Y	Case Z
Current Ratio			
Acid-Test Ratio			

Interpretation

Chapter 4 Exercise 4-13 ***Name*** ______________________

(a) PERIODIC

GENERAL JOURNAL

Date		Account Titles and Explanation	P. R.	Debit	Credit

(a) PERPETUAL

GENERAL JOURNAL

Date		Account Titles and Explanation	P. R.	Debit	Credit

Chapter 4 Exercise 4-14 *Name* ______________________

GENERAL JOURNAL

Date		Account Titles and Explanation	P. R.	Debit	Credit

 Name ______________________________

(1) BUYER

GENERAL JOURNAL

Date		Account Titles and Explanation	P. R.	Debit	Credit

(2) SELLER

GENERAL JOURNAL

Date		Account Titles and Explanation	P. R.	Debit	Credit

Chapter 4 Exercise 4-16 *Name* ______________________

(1) BUYER

GENERAL JOURNAL

Date		Account Titles and Explanation	P. R.	Debit	Credit

(2) SELLER

GENERAL JOURNAL

Date		Account Titles and Explanation	P. R.	Debit	Credit

GENERAL JOURNAL

Date		Account Titles and Explanation	P. R.	Debit	Credit

 Name ______________________________

GENERAL JOURNAL

Date		Account Titles and Explanation	P. R.	Debit	Credit

GENERAL JOURNAL

Date		Account Titles and Explanation	P. R.	Debit	Credit

 Name ____________________

GENERAL JOURNAL

Date		Account Titles and Explanation	P. R.	Debit	Credit

Chapter 4 Problem 4-3A or 4-3B *Name* ____________________

Part 1

GENERAL JOURNAL

Date		Account Titles and Explanation	P. R.	Debit	Credit

Part 2

Income Statement

Income Statement

Part 4

 Name ______________________

Part 1

Part 2

Chapter 4 Problem 4-4A or 4-4B *Name* ____________________
Part 3 (Continued)

Income Statement

Part 4

Income Statement

Chapter 4 Problem 4-5A or 4-5B *Name* ______________________

Part 1 Closing Entries

GENERAL JOURNAL

Date		Account Titles and Explanation	P. R.	Debit	Credit

Chapter 4 Problem 4-5A or 4-5B Name ______________________
Part 2 (Continued)

Part 3

Chapter 4 Problem 4-6A or 4-6B

Name ______________________

______________, Company

Work Sheet

For Year Ended ______________

Account Title	Unadjusted Trial Balance		Adjustments		Adjusted Trial Balance		Income Statement		Balance Sheet	
	Dr.	Cr.	Dr.	Cr.	Dr.	Cr.	Dr.	Cr.	Dr.	Cr.

Chapter 4 Serial Problem Name ______________________

Part 1 Success Systems

Journal Entries

GENERAL JOURNAL

Date		Account Titles and Explanation	P. R.	Debit	Credit

Chapter 4 Serial Problem *Name* ______________________

Part 1 Success Systems

Journal Entries (Continued)

Date		Account Titles and Explanation	P. R.	Debit	Credit

Chapter 4 Serial Problem *Name* ______________________

Part 1 Success Systems

Journal Entries (Continued)

Date		Account Titles and Explanation	P. R.	Debit	Credit

Chapter 4 Serial Problem *Name* ______________________

Part 1 Success Systems

Journal Entries (Continued)

Date		Account Titles and Explanation	P. R.	Debit	Credit

Chapter 4 Serial Problem *Name* ______________________________

Part 2 Success Systems

(Continued)

GENERAL LEDGER

Cash **ACCOUNT NO. 101**

Date	Explanation	P.R.	DEBIT	CREDIT	BALANCE
2004 Dec. 31	Balance				58,160

Chapter 4 Serial Problem Name ______________________
Part 2 Success Systems
(Continued)

Accounts Receivable - Alex's Engineering Co. ACCOUNT NO. 106.1

Date	Explanation	P.R.	DEBIT	CREDIT	BALANCE
2004 Dec. 31	Balance				0

Accounts Receivable - Wildcat Services ACCOUNT NO. 106.2

Date	Explanation	P.R.	DEBIT	CREDIT	BALANCE
2004 Dec. 31	Balance				0

Accounts Receivable - Easy Leasing ACCOUNT NO. 106.3

Date	Explanation	P.R.	DEBIT	CREDIT	BALANCE
2004 Dec. 31	Balance				0

Accounts Receivable - Clark Co. ACCOUNT NO. 106.4

Date	Explanation	P.R.	DEBIT	CREDIT	BALANCE
2004 Dec. 31	Balance				3,000

Chapter 4 Serial Problem Name ______________________
Part 2 Success Systems
(Continued)

Accounts Receivable - Chang Corporation ACCOUNT NO. 106.5

Date	Explanation	P.R.	DEBIT	CREDIT	BALANCE
2004 Dec. 31	Balance				0

Accounts Receivable - Gomez Co. ACCOUNT NO. 106.6

Date	Explanation	P.R.	DEBIT	CREDIT	BALANCE
2004 Dec. 31	Balance				2,668

Accounts Receivable - Delta Co. ACCOUNT NO. 106.7

Date	Explanation	P.R.	DEBIT	CREDIT	BALANCE
2004 Dec. 31	Balance				0

Accounts Receivable - KC, Inc. ACCOUNT NO. 106.8

Date	Explanation	P.R.	DEBIT	CREDIT	BALANCE
2004 Dec. 31	Balance				0

Accounts Receivable - Dream, Inc. ACCOUNT NO. 106.9

Date	Explanation	P.R.	DEBIT	CREDIT	BALANCE
2004 Dec. 31	Balance				0

Chapter 4 Serial Problem Name ______________________

Part 2 Success Systems (Continued)

Merchandise Inventory ACCOUNT NO. 119

Date	Explanation	P.R.	DEBIT	CREDIT	BALANCE
2004 Dec. 31	Balance				0

Computer Supplies ACCOUNT NO. 126

Date	Explanation	P.R.	DEBIT	CREDIT	BALANCE
2004 Dec. 31	Balance				580

Prepaid Insurance ACCOUNT NO. 128

Date	Explanation	P.R.	DEBIT	CREDIT	BALANCE
2004 Dec. 31	Balance				1,665

Chapter 4 Serial Problem *Name* ____________________
Part 2 Success Systems
(Continued)

Prepaid Rent ACCOUNT NO. 131

Date	Explanation	P.R.	DEBIT	CREDIT	BALANCE
2004 Dec. 31	Balance				825

Office Equipment ACCOUNT NO. 163

Date	Explanation	P.R.	DEBIT	CREDIT	BALANCE
2004 Dec. 31	Balance				8,000

Accumulated Depreciation - Office Equipment ACCOUNT NO. 164

Date	Explanation	P.R.	DEBIT	CREDIT	BALANCE
2004 Dec. 31	Balance				400

Computer Equipment ACCOUNT NO. 167

Date	Explanation	P.R.	DEBIT	CREDIT	BALANCE
2004 Dec. 31	Balance				20,000

Accumulated Depreciation - Computer Equipment ACCOUNT NO. 168

Date	Explanation	P.R.	DEBIT	CREDIT	BALANCE
2004 Dec. 31	Balance				1,250

Chapter 4 Part 2 — Serial Problem: Success Systems (Continued)   *Name* ______________________

Accounts Payable — ACCOUNT NO. 201

Date	Explanation	P.R.	DEBIT	CREDIT	BALANCE
2004 Dec. 31	Balance				1,100

Wages Payable — ACCOUNT NO. 210

Date	Explanation	P.R.	DEBIT	CREDIT	BALANCE
2004 Dec. 31	Balance				500

Unearned Computer Services Revenue — ACCOUNT NO. 236

Date	Explanation	P.R.	DEBIT	CREDIT	BALANCE
2004 Dec. 31	Balance				1,500

Common Stock — ACCOUNT NO. 307

Date	Explanation	P.R.	DEBIT	CREDIT	BALANCE
2004 Dec. 31	Balance				83,000

Retained Earnings — ACCOUNT NO. 318

Date	Explanation	P.R.	DEBIT	CREDIT	BALANCE
2004 Dec. 31	Balance				7,148

Chapter 4 Serial Problem *Name* ______________________
Part 2 Success Systems
(Continued)

Dividends ACCOUNT NO. 319

Date	Explanation	P.R.	DEBIT	CREDIT	BALANCE

Computer Services Revenue ACCOUNT NO. 403

Date	Explanation	P.R.	DEBIT	CREDIT	BALANCE

Sales ACCOUNT NO. 413

Date	Explanation	P.R.	DEBIT	CREDIT	BALANCE

Sales Returns and Allowances ACCOUNT NO. 414

Date	Explanation	P.R.	DEBIT	CREDIT	BALANCE

Chapter 4 Serial Problem *Name* ______________________

Part 2 Success Systems (Continued)

Sales Discounts — ACCOUNT NO. 415

Date	Explanation	P.R.	DEBIT	CREDIT	BALANCE

Cost of Goods Sold — ACCOUNT NO. 502

Date	Explanation	P.R.	DEBIT	CREDIT	BALANCE

Depreciation Expense-Office Equipment — ACCOUNT NO. 612

Date	Explanation	P.R.	DEBIT	CREDIT	BALANCE

Depreciation Expense-Computer Equipment — ACCOUNT NO. 613

Date	Explanation	P.R.	DEBIT	CREDIT	BALANCE

Wages Expense — ACCOUNT NO. 623

Date	Explanation	P.R.	DEBIT	CREDIT	BALANCE

Chapter 4 Serial Problem *Name* ____________________
Part 2 Success Systems
(Continued)

Insurance Expense ACCOUNT NO. 637

Date	Explanation	P.R.	DEBIT	CREDIT	BALANCE

Rent Expense ACCOUNT NO. 640

Date	Explanation	P.R.	DEBIT	CREDIT	BALANCE

Computer Supplies Expense ACCOUNT NO. 652

Date	Explanation	P.R.	DEBIT	CREDIT	BALANCE

Advertising Expense ACCOUNT NO. 655

Date	Explanation	P.R.	DEBIT	CREDIT	BALANCE

Mileage Expense ACCOUNT NO. 676

Date	Explanation	P.R.	DEBIT	CREDIT	BALANCE

Miscellaneous Expense ACCOUNT NO. 677

Date	Explanation	P.R.	DEBIT	CREDIT	BALANCE

Repairs Expense - Computer ACCOUNT NO. 684

Date	Explanation	P.R.	DEBIT	CREDIT	BALANCE

Name ______________________________

SUCCESS SYSTEMS
Partial Work Sheet
March 31, 2005

Acct. No.	ACCOUNT TITLES	UNADJUSTED TRIAL BALANCE		ADJUSTMENTS		ADJUSTED TRIAL BALANCE	
		Dr.	Cr.	Dr.	Cr.	Dr.	Cr.

Name ____________________

SUCCESS SYSTEMS
Income Statement
For Three Months Ended March 31, 2005

Part 5

SUCCESS SYSTEMS
Statement of Retained Earnings
For Three Months Ended March 31, 2005

Chapter 4 Serial Problem Name ______________________

Part 6 Success Systems (Continued)

SUCCESS SYSTEMS
Balance Sheet
March 31, 2005

Chapter 4 Reporting in Action--BTN 4-1 *Name* ____________________

Part 1

Part 2

Part 3

Roll On:

Chapter 4 Comparative Analysis Name ______________________

BTN 4-2

Part 1

Part 2

Part 3

Chapter 4 Ethics Challenge-BTN 4-3 *Name* ______________________

Part 1

Part 2

Name ______________________________

MEMORANDUM

TO:
FROM:
SUBJECT:
DATE:

 Name ______________________

	2003	2002	2001	2000
Fiscal Year				
Revenues				
Cost of goods sold				
Gross margin				
Gross margin ratio				

Analysis:

 Name ________________________

BTN 4-6

(1a)

(1b)

(1c)

(1d)

 Name ______________________

(1e)

(2)

Check: Net Income is ______________.

(3)

Chapter 4 *Business Week* Activity **Name** ______________________

BTN 4-7

(1)

(2)

(3)

(4)

(5)

Name ______________________

Damani Dada
Forecasted Income Statement
For Year Ended April 30, 2006

Part 2

Part 3

 Name ______________________________

Chapter 4 Global Decision--BTN 4-10 *Name* ____________________

(1)

(2)

(3)

 Name ______________________

a) FIFO

Date	Purchases	Cost of Goods Sold	Inventory Balance

b) LIFO

Date	Purchases	Cost of Goods Sold	Inventory Balance

c) Weighted Average

Date	Purchases	Cost of Goods Sold	Inventory Balance

d) Specific Identification

Chapter 5 Quick Study 5-2 *Name* ______________________

Quick Study 5-3

b) FIFO

Date	Purchases	Cost of Goods Sold	Inventory Balance

c) LIFO

Date	Purchases	Cost of Goods Sold	Inventory Balance

c) Weighted Average

Date	Purchases	Cost of Goods Sold	Inventory Balance

Quick Study 5-4

(1) ______
(2) ______
(3) ______
(4) ______
(5) ______

Quick Study 5-5

(1) ______

(2) ______

Chapter 5 Quick Study 5-6 *Name* ______________________

Quick Study 5-7

Quick Study 5-8

Quick Study 5-9

Inventory Items	Units	Per Unit Cost	Per Unit Market	Total Cost	Total Market	LCM applied to: Items	LCM applied to: Whole

Chapter 5 Quick Study 5-10 *Name* ______________________

(a) ______________________

____

(b) ______________________

____

(c) ______________________

____

(d) ______________________

____

(e) ______________________

____

(f) ______________________

____

Quick Study 5-11

____

____

____

____

____

____

____

____

Quick Study 5-12[A]

(a) ______________________

____

____

(b) ______________________

____

____

(c) ______________________

____

____

(d) ______________________

____

____

Chapter 5 Quick Study 5-13[A] *Name* ______________________

(a)

(b)

(c)

Quick Study 5-14[B]

Exercise 5-1

(a) Specific Identification

(b) Weighted Average Perpetual

Date	Purchases	Cost of Goods Sold	Inventory Balance

Chapter 5 Exercise 5-1 (Continued) *Name* ____________________

(c) FIFO Perpetual

Date	Purchases	Cost of Goods Sold	Inventory Balance

(d) LIFO Perpetual

Date	Purchases	Cost of Goods Sold	Inventory Balance

 Name ______________________

LAKIA CORPORATION
Income Statements
For Year Ended December 31, 2005

	Specific Identification	Weighted Average	FIFO	LIFO

(1)

(2)

(3)

Chapter 5 Exercise 5-3 *Name* ____________________

(a) FIFO Perpetual

Date	Purchases	Cost of Goods Sold	Inventory Balance

FIFO Gross Margin:

(a) LIFO Perpetual

Date	Purchases	Cost of Goods Sold	Inventory Balance

LIFO Gross Margin:

Chapter 5 Exercise 5-4 *Name* ______________________

Specific Identification Method

(a) Ending Inventory and Cost of Goods Sold:

(b) Gross Margin:

Chapter 5 Exercise 5-5 *Name* ______________________________

Inventory Items	Units	Per Unit Cost	Per Unit Market	Total Cost	Total Market	LCM applied to: Products	LCM applied to: Whole

(a) LCM applied to whole: ______________________________

(b) LCM applied to products: ______________________________

Exercise 5-6

(1) Gross Profit

____

____

____

(2)

	2004	2005	2006
Sales			
Cost of goods sold:			
Beginning inventory			
Cost of Purchases			
Ending Inventory			
Cost of goods sold			
Gross Profit			

Chapter 5 Exercise 5-7 *Name* ______________________

Inventory Turnover (2004):

Inventory Turnover (2005):

Days' Sales in Inventory (2004):

Days' Sales in Inventory (2005):

Analysis Comments:

Chapter 5 Exercise 5-8 *Name* ______________________

(1) (a)

(b)

(2)

Chapter 5 Exercise 5-9[A] *Name* ____________________

Method and Computations	Ending Inventory	Cost of Goods Sold
(a) Specific Identification		
(b) Weighted Average Periodic		
(c) FIFO Periodic		
(d) LIFO Periodic		

Chapter 5 Exercise 5-10A Name ______________________

Method and Computations	Ending Inventory	Cost of Goods Sold
(a) FIFO Periodic		
(b) LIFO Periodic		

(c) FIFO Gross Margin:

LIFO Gross Margin

Chapter 5 Exercise 5-11[A] *Name* ______________________

Method and Computations	Ending Inventory	Cost of Goods Sold
(a) Specific Identification		
(b) Weighted Average Periodic		
(c) FIFO Periodic		
(d) LIFO Periodic		

Income Effect(s):

Chapter 5 Exercise 5-12A Name ______________________

Method and Computations	Ending Inventory	Cost of Goods Sold
(a) Specific Identification		
(b) Weighted Average Periodic		
(c) FIFO Periodic		
(d) LIFO Periodic		

Income Effect(s):

Chapter 5 Exercise 5-13[B] *Name* ____________________

	At Cost	At Retail

Exercise 5-14[B]

 Name ______________________

(1) Cost of Goods Available for Sale and Units Available for Sale:

(2) Ending Inventory (in Units):

Chapter 5 Problem 5-1A or 5-1B (Continued) *Name* ______________________

(3a) FIFO Perpetual

Date	Purchases	Cost of Goods Sold	Inventory Balance

Chapter 5 Problem 5-1A or 5-1B (Continued) *Name* ____________________

(3b) LIFO Perpetual

Date	Purchases	Cost of Goods Sold	Inventory Balance

(3c) Specific Identification

 Name ____________________

(3d) Weighted Average Perpetual

Date	Purchases	Cost of Goods Sold	Inventory Balance

(4) Gross Profit

	FIFO	LIFO	Specific Identification	Weighted Average
Sales				
Cost of goods sold				
Gross profit				

(5)

Chapter 5 Problem 5-2A or 5-2B *Name* ______________________

Part 1

(a) Cost of Goods Sold	*2004*	*2005*	*2006*
Reported...............................			
Adjustments: 12/31/2004 error			
Adjustments: 12/31/2005 error			
Corrected..............................			

(b) Net Income	*2004*	*2005*	*2006*
Reported...............................			
Adjustments: 12/31/2004 error			
Adjustments: 12/31/2005 error			
Corrected..............................			

(c) Total Current Assets	*2004*	*2005*	*2006*
Reported...............................			
Adjustments: 12/31/2004 error			
Adjustments: 12/31/2005 error			
Corrected..............................			

(d) Equity	*2004*	*2005*	*2006*
Reported...............................			
Adjustments: 12/31/2004 error			
Adjustments: 12/31/2005 error			
Corrected..............................			

Part 2

Part 3

Chapter 5 Problem 5-3A or 5-3B *Name* ____________________

Inventory		Per Unit		Total	Total	LCM applied to :		
Items	Units	Cost	Market	Cost	Market	Items	Categories	Whole

(a)

(b)

(c)

Chapter 5 Problem 5-4A or 5-4B *Name* ______________________

Part 1

Units Available for Sale and Cost of Units Available for Sale:

Part 2

(a) FIFO Periodic

(b) LIFO Periodic

(C) Weighted Average Periodic

Chapter 5 Problem 5-5A or 5-5B *Name* ____________________

Part 1

Comparative Income Statements

____

Income Statements Comparing FIFO, LIFO and Weighted Average
For Year Ended December 31, 2005

	FIFO	LIFO	Weighted Average

Supporting Calculations:

Chapter 5 Problem 5-5A or 5-5B *Name* ______________________
Part 2 (Continued)

Part 3

Advantages:

LIFO

FIFO

Disadvantages:

LIFO

FIFO

Chapter 5 Problem 5-6A or 5-6B *Name* ______________________

Part 1

____________ Company Estimated Inventory December 31	At Cost	At Retail

Part 2

____________ Company Inventory Shortage December 31	At Cost	At Retail

____________ Company Estimated Inventory March 31	At Cost	At Retail

Chapter 5 Serial Problem *Name* ____________________

Success Systems

Part 1

Inventory Turnover:

Days' Sales in Inventory:

Part 2

Analysis:

Reporting in Action--BTN 5-1

(1)

(2) 2003:

2002:

(3)

 Name ______________________

(4)

(5)

(a) Inventory Turnover:

(b) Days' Sales in Inventory:

(6) Roll On:

Chapter 5 Comparative Analysis *Name* ______________________

BTN 5-2

(1)

Inventory Turnover--Krispy Kreme:

Inventory Turnover--Tastykake:

(2)

Days' Sales in Inventory - Krispy Kreme:

Days' Sales in Inventory - Tastykake:

(3) Interpretation:

Chapter 5 Ethics Challenge--BTN 5-3 *Name* ______________________

(1) Profit Margin:

Current Ratio:

(2)

 Name ____________________

MEMORANDUM

TO:
FROM:
SUBJECT:
DATE:

Chapter 5 Taking It to the Net *Name* ____________________
BTN 5-5

(1)

(2)

(3) Gross Margin:

Gross Margin Ratio:

(4)

Inventory Turnover:

Days' Sales in Inventory

Teamwork in Action--BTN 5-6

(a) and (b) Concept discussion:

 Name ______________________

(a) and (b) Procedures:

Date	Purchases	Cost of Goods Sold	Inventory Balance

(c)

(d)

(e)

Chapter 5 *Business Week* Activity **Name** ______________________

BTN 5-7

(1)

(2)

(3)

(4)

Entrepreneurial Decision--BTN 5-8

(1)(a)

(b)

(2)

Chapter 5 Hitting the Road *Name* ______________________

BTN 5-9

Global Decision--BTN 5-10

(1) Inventory Turnover--Grupo Bimbo:

Days' Sales in Inventory--Grupo Bimbo:

(2) Interpretation:

 Quick Study 6-1 *Name* ______________________________

(1)

(2)

(3)

Quick Study 6-2

(1) (a)

(b)

(c)

(2)

Quick Study 6-3

(1)

(2)

 Quick Study 6-4 *Name* ______________________

(1) ______________________

(2) ______________________

(3) ______________________

Quick Study 6-5

(1)

GENERAL JOURNAL

Date		Account Titles and Explanation	P. R.	Debit	Credit
(a) Establishment of the Fund:					
(b) Reimbursement of the Fund at Month-End:					

(2) ______________________

Chapter 6 Quick Study 6-6 *Name* ______________________

Parts 1 and 2

(1)		(2)
Bank or Book Effect	Add or Subtract	Journal Entry Required or Not
(a)		
(b)		
(c)		
(d)		
(e)		
(f)		
(g)		

Quick Study 6-7

Days' Sales Uncollected (2005):

Days' Sales Uncollected (2004):

Interpretation and Explanation:

Quick Study 6-8

(a)

(b)

Chapter 6 Exercise 6-1 *Name* ______________________

(1)

(2)

Exercise 6-2

(a) Internal Control Problems:

(b) Internal Control Recommendations:

Exercise 6-3

Evaluation:

Principles Ignored:

 Name ____________________

(1) Establish the Fund

GENERAL JOURNAL

Date		Account Titles and Explanation	P. R.	Debit	Credit

(2) Reimburse and Reduce the Fund

GENERAL JOURNAL

Date		Account Titles and Explanation	P.R.	Debit	Credit

Chapter 6 Exercise 6-5 *Name* ____________________

(1) Establish the Fund

GENERAL JOURNAL

Date		Account Titles and Explanation	P. R.	Debit	Credit

(2) Reimburse the Fund

GENERAL JOURNAL

Date		Account Titles and Explanation	P. R.	Debit	Credit

(3) Reimburse and Increase the Fund

GENERAL JOURNAL

Date		Account Titles and Explanation	P. R.	Debit	Credit

Chapter 6 Exercise 6-6 *Name* ______________________

	Bank Balance		Book Balance			Not Shown on the Reconciliation
	Add	Deduct	Add	Deduct	Adjust	
1. Bank service charge.						
2. Checks written and mailed to payees on October 2.						
3. Check written by another depositor but charged against the company's account.						
4. Principle and interest collected by the bank but not recorded by the company.						
5. Special charge for collection of note in part 4 on company's behalf.						
6. Check written against the company account and cleared by the bank; erroneously omitted by the company's recordkeeper.						
7. Interest earned on the account.						
8. Deposit made on September 30 after the bank closed.						
9. Checks outstanding on August 31 that cleared the bank in September.						
10. NSF check from customer returned on September 25 but not recorded by the company						
11. Checks written and mailed to payees on September 30.						
12. Deposit made on September 5 and processed on September 8.						

Chapter 6 Exercise 6-7 *Name* ______________________

(1) ______________________

(2) ______________________

(3) ______________________

Exercise 6-8

Bank Reconciliation

Exercise 6-9

GENERAL JOURNAL

Date		Account Titles and Explanation	P. R.	Debit	Credit

 Name ______________________________

Days' Sales Uncollected (2004):

Days' Sales Uncollected (2005):

Interpretation of Change:

 Name ______________________________

Chapter 6 Exercise 6-12[B] *Name* ______________________________

(a) Recording Invoices at Gross Amounts--Gross Method

GENERAL JOURNAL

Date		Account Titles and Explanation	P. R.	Debit	Credit

(a) Recording Invoices at Net Amounts--Net Method

GENERAL JOURNAL

Date		Account Titles and Explanation	P. R.	Debit	Credit

(1) Principle Violated:
Recommended

(2) Principle Violated:
Recommended

(3) Principle Violated:
Recommended

(4) Principle Violated:
Recommended

(5) Principle Violated:
Recommended

Chapter 6 Problem 6-2A or 6-2B *Name* ____________________

Part 1

GENERAL JOURNAL

Date		Account Titles and Explanation	P. R.	Debit	Credit

Part 2

Chapter 6 Problem 6-3A or 6-3B *Name* ____________________

Part 1

GENERAL JOURNAL

Date		Account Titles and Explanation	P. R.	Debit	Credit

Part 2

Petty Cash Payments Report

Part 3

GENERAL JOURNAL

Date		Account Titles and Explanation	P.R.	Debit	Credit

Chapter 6 Problem 6-4A or 6-4B *Name* ______________________

Part 1

Bank Reconciliation

Part 2

GENERAL JOURNAL

Date		Account Titles and Explanation	P. R.	Debit	Credit

(a)

(b)

Problem 6-5A or 6-5B
Part 1

Bank Reconciliation

Chapter 6 Problem 6-5A or 6-5B *Name* ______________________

Part 2 (Continued)

GENERAL JOURNAL

Date		Account Titles and Explanation	P. R.	Debit	Credit

Part 3

(1) ______________________

(2) ______________________

(3) ______________________

Chapter 6 **Serial Problem** *Name* ______________________

Part 1 **Success Systems**

Bank Reconciliation

Part 2

GENERAL JOURNAL

Date		Account Titles and Explanation	P. R.	Debit	Credit

Chapter 6 Reporting in Action--BTN 6-1 *Name* ______________________________

Part 1

	Feb. 2, 2003		Feb. 3, 2002	
Item	Balance ($)	Cash & Equiv. as % of Balance	Balance ($)	Cash & Equiv. as % of Balance

Interpretation:

Part 2

Name ______________________

Days' Sales Uncollected (Feb. 2, 2003):

Days' Sales Uncollected (Feb. 3, 2002):

Interpretation:

Part 4

Roll On:

 Name ______________________

BTN 6-2

Krispy Kreme:

Days' Sales Uncollected (Current year):

Days' Sales Uncollected (Prior year):

Interpretation:

Tastykake:

Days' Sales Uncollected (Current year):

Days' Sales Uncollected (Prior year):

Interpretation:

Comparison - Krisky Kreme vs. Tastykake:

Chapter 6 Ethics Challenge--BTN 6-3 *Name* ____________________

(1)

(2)

(3)

(4)

Name ______________________________

MEMORANDUM

TO:
FROM:
SUBJECT:
DATE:

Chapter 6 Taking It to the Net *Name* ______________________________

BTN 6-5

(1) ______________________________

(2) ______________________________

(3) ______________________________

(4) ______________________________

(5) ______________________________

(6) ______________________________

(7) ______________________________

(8) ______________________________

(9) ______________________________

(10) ______________________________

(11) ______________________________

(12) ______________________________

Chapter 6 Teamwork in Action--BTN 6-6 *Name* ______________________

(1) ______________________

(2) ______________________

(3) ______________________

(4) ______________________

(5) ______________________

(6) ______________________

(7) ______________________

(8) ______________________

(9) ______________________

(10) ______________________

(11) ______________________

Chapter 6 Business Week Activity *Name* ____________________

BTN 6-7

(1)

(2)

(3)

(4)

(5)

Chapter 6 Entrepreneurial Decision *Name* ______________________

BTN 6-8

(1) ______________________

(2) ______________________

(3) ______________________

(4) ______________________

(5) ______________________

(6) ______________________

(7) ______________________

Hitting the Road--BTN 6-9

Chapter 6 Global Decision--BTN 6-10 ***Name*** ______________________

1. ______________________

2. ______________________

3. ______________________

4. ______________________

5. ______________________

6. ______________________

 Name ____________________

(1)

GENERAL JOURNAL

Date		Account Titles and Explanation	P. R.	Debit	Credit

(2)

GENERAL JOURNAL

Date		Account Titles and Explanation	P. R.	Debit	Credit

 Name ______________________________

(1)

GENERAL JOURNAL

Date		Account Titles and Explanation	P. R.	Debit	Credit

(2)

GENERAL JOURNAL

Date		Account Titles and Explanation	P. R.	Debit	Credit

(1)

GENERAL JOURNAL

Date		Account Titles and Explanation	P. R.	Debit	Credit

(2) ______________________

____

____

(3)

GENERAL JOURNAL

Date		Account Titles and Explanation	P. R.	Debit	Credit

Quick Study 7-4

GENERAL JOURNAL

Date		Account Titles and Explanation	P. R.	Debit	Credit

 Quick Study 7-5 *Name* ______________________________

GENERAL JOURNAL

Date		Account Titles and Explanation	P. R.	Debit	Credit

Quick Study 7-6

Accounts Receivable Turnover:

Interpretation:

GENERAL JOURNAL

Date		Account Titles and Explanation	P. R.	Debit	Credit

Chapter 7 Exercise 7-2 *Name* ______________________

Part 1

GENERAL LEDGER

Accounts Receivable		Sales		Sales Returns and Allowances	

ACCOUNTS RECEIVABLE LEDGER

Surf Shop		Yum Enterprises		Matt Albin	

Part 2

Schedule of Accounts Receivable

Comparison:

 Name ______________________________

GENERAL JOURNAL

Date		Account Titles and Explanation	P. R.	Debit	Credit

(a)

GENERAL JOURNAL

Date		Account Titles and Explanation	P. R.	Debit	Credit

(b)

GENERAL JOURNAL

Date		Account Titles and Explanation	P. R.	Debit	Credit

 Name ______________________

GENERAL JOURNAL

Date		Account Titles and Explanation	P. R.	Debit	Credit

Financial Statement Note(s):

 Name ______________________

GENERAL JOURNAL

Date		Account Titles and Explanation	P. R.	Debit	Credit

Chapter 7 Exercise 7-7 *Name* ______________________________

GENERAL JOURNAL

Date		Account Titles and Explanation	P. R.	Debit	Credit

 Name ______________________________

GENERAL JOURNAL

Date		Account Titles and Explanation	P. R.	Debit	Credit

Chapter 7 Exercise 7-9 *Name* ______________________

Accounts Receivable Turnover (2004):

Accounts Receivable Turnover (2005):

Comparison and Interpretation:

Chapter 7 Problem 7-1A or 7-2B *Name* ____________________

GENERAL JOURNAL

Date		Account Titles and Explanation	P. R.	Debit	Credit

Chapter 7 Problem 7-2A or 7-2B *Name* ____________________

2004

GENERAL JOURNAL

Date		Account Titles and Explanation	P. R.	Debit	Credit

Supporting work:

Chapter 7 Problem 7-2A or 7-2B *Name* ______________________

2005

GENERAL JOURNAL

Date		Account Titles and Explanation	P. R.	Debit	Credit

Supporting work:

Chapter 7 Problem 7-3A or 7-3B *Name* ____________________

Part 1

GENERAL JOURNAL

Date		Account Titles and Explanation	P. R.	Debit	Credit
(a)					
(b)					
(c)					

Part 2

Problem 7-4A or 7-4B

Part 1

Part 2

GENERAL JOURNAL

Date		Account Titles and Explanation	P. R.	Debit	Credit

Part 3

Chapter 7 **Problem 7-5A or 7-5B** ***Name*** ____________________

Part 1 **Preparation Component**

Date		Account Titles and Explanation	P. R.	Debit	Credit
2004					
2005					

Chapter 7 Problem 7-5A or 7-5B *Name* ______________________
Part 1 (Continued)

Date		Account Titles and Explanation	P. R.	Debit	Credit

Part 2

Reporting:

Reasoning:

Principle:

Chapter 7 Serial Problem *Name* ______________________________

Part 1 Success Systems

GENERAL JOURNAL

Date		Account Titles and Explanation	P. R.	Debit	Credit
(a)					
(b)					

Part 2

GENERAL JOURNAL

Date		Account Titles and Explanation	P. R.	Debit	Credit

Part 3

Chapter 7 Reporting in Action--BTN 7-1 *Name* ______________________

(1)

(2) Liquid Assets as a percent of Current Liabilities (Feb. 2, 2003):

Liquid Assets as a percent of Current Liabilities (Feb. 3, 2002):

Comparison and Interpretation:

(3)

(4) Accounts Receivable Turnover (2003):

(5) Roll On:

Chapter 7 Comparative Analysis *Name* ______________________

BTN 7-2

(1) Krispy Kreme's Accounts Receivable Turnover (Current Year and Prior Year):

Tastykake's Accounts Receivable Turnover (Current Year and Prior Year):

(2) Krispy Kreme's Average Collection Period (Current Year and Prior Year):

Tastykake's Average Collection Period (Current Year and Prior Year):

(3) Efficiency Comparison:

(4) Krispy Kreme's Percent of Uncollectibles (Current Year and Prior Year)

Tastykake's Percent of Uncollectibles (Current Year and Prior Year)

Comparison:

Chapter 7 Ethics Challenge--BTN 7-3 ***Name*** ____________________

(1)

(2)

(3)

 Name ______________________

MEMORANDUM

TO:

FROM:

SUBJECT:

DATE:

Chapter 7 Taking It to the Net--BTN 7-5 *Name* ______________________

(1)

(2)

Chapter 7 Teamwork in Action--BTN 7-6 *Name* ______________________

Estimate of Uncollectibles:

Adjusting Entry:

GENERAL JOURNAL

Date		Account Titles and Explanation	P. R.	Debit	Credit

Presentation of Net Realizable Accounts Receivable in Balance Sheet:

Chapter 7 *Business Week Activity* BTN 7-7 *Name* ______________________

(1)

(2)

(3)

(4)

Chapter 7 Entrepreneurial Decision *Name* ______________________

Part 1 BTN 7-8

Added Monthly Net Income (Loss) under Plan A

Added Monthly Net Income (Loss) under Plan B

Part 2

 Name ____________________

Global Decision--BTN 7-10

(1)

(2)

Chapter 8 Quick Study 8-1 *Name* ______________________________

Quick Study 8-2

(1)

(2)

(3)

Quick Study 8-3

(1) Straight-line:

(2) Units-of-Production:

Quick Study 8-4

Revised Straight-Line Depreciation:

Chapter 8 Quick Study 8-5 *Name* ____________________

First Year:

Second Year:

Third Year:

Quick Study 8-6

(1)

(a)

(b)

(c)

(d)

(2)

GENERAL JOURNAL

Date		Account Titles and Explanation	P. R.	Debit	Credit
(a)					
(b)					

 Quick Study 8-7 *Name* ____________________

GENERAL JOURNAL

Date		Account Titles and Explanation	P. R.	Debit	Credit
(1)					
(2)					

Quick Study 8-8

GENERAL JOURNAL

Date		Account Titles and Explanation	P. R.	Debit	Credit
(1)					
(2)					

 Quick Study 8-9 *Name* ______________________

Intangible Assets(s): ______________________

____

Natural Resources(s): ______________________

____

Quick Study 8-10

GENERAL JOURNAL

Date		Account Titles and Explanation	P. R.	Debit	Credit
(1)					
(2)					

Quick Study 8-11

Total Asset Turnover: ______________________

____

____

Interpretation: ______________________

____

____

Chapter 8 Exercise 8-1 *Name* ______________________________

Total Cost to be Recorded:

Exercise 8-2

Cost of Assets:

GENERAL JOURNAL

Date		Account Titles and Explanation	P. R.	Debit	Credit

Chapter 8 Exercise 8-3 **Name** ______________________

Allocation of Costs to Assets:

GENERAL JOURNAL

Date		Account Titles and Explanation	P. R.	Debit	Credit

Chapter 8 Exercise 8-4 *Name* ______________________________

(1) Straight-Line Depreciation:

Year	Annual Depreciation	Year-End Book Value

(2) Double-Declining-Balance Depreciation:

Year	Beginning-Year Book Value	Depreciation Rate	Annual Depreciation	Year-End Book Value

Chapter 8 Exercise 8-5 *Name* ______________________________

(1) Straight-Line:

(2) Units-of-Production:

(3) Double-Declining-Balance:

Exercise 8-6

(1) Straight-Line:

(2) Double-Declining-Balance:

 Name ______________________

(1) ______________________

(2) ______________________

Chapter 8 Exercise 8-8 *Name* ______________________

(1) Straight-Line Depreciation:

Year	Income before Depreciation	Depreciation Expense	Net Income

(2) Double-Declining-Balance Depreciation:

Year	Income before Depreciation	Depreciation Expense	Net Income

Chapter 8 Exercise 8-9 *Name* ______________________

(1) ______________________

(2)

GENERAL JOURNAL

Date		Account Titles and Explanation	P. R.	Debit	Credit

(3) ______________________

(4)

GENERAL JOURNAL

Date		Account Titles and Explanation	P. R.	Debit	Credit

 Exercise 8-10 *Name* ____________________

GENERAL JOURNAL

Date		Account Titles and Explanation	P. R.	Debit	Credit
(1)					
(2)					
(3)					

Exercise 8-11

(1) ____________________

(2) ____________________

(3) ____________________

GENERAL JOURNAL

Date		Account Titles and Explanation	P. R.	Debit	Credit
(1)					
(2)					
(3)					

Chapter 8 Exercise 8-13 *Name* ______________________________

GENERAL JOURNAL

Date		Account Titles and Explanation	P. R.	Debit	Credit
(1)					
(2)					

Computations:

Exercise 8-14

GENERAL JOURNAL

Date		Account Titles and Explanation	P. R.	Debit	Credit

Chapter 8 Exercise 8-15 *Name* ______________________

GENERAL JOURNAL

Date		Account Titles and Explanation	P. R.	Debit	Credit

Exercise 8-16

(1) Value of Goodwill:

(2) Value of Goodwill:

Exercise 8-17

(1)

(2)

(3)

 Name ______________________

Total Asset Turnover (2004):

Total Asset Turnover (2005):

Efficiency Analysis:

Chapter 8 Problem 8-1A or 8-1B *Name* ______________________

Part 1

	Appraised Value	Percent of Total	Apportioned Cost
Building..........................			
Land...............................			
Land Improvments.............			
Vehicles (or Trucks)...........			
Total...............................			

GENERAL JOURNAL

Date		Account Titles and Explanation	P. R.	Debit	Credit

Part 2

Part 3

Part 4

Chapter 8 Problem 8-2A or 8-2B *Name* ______________________
Part 1 (Continued)

	Land	Building 2 (or B)	Building 3 (or C)	Land Improv. 1 (or B)	Land Improv. 2 (or C)
Purchase price.........					
Demolition...............					
Land grading............					
New building............					
New improvements...					
Totals......................					

Computations:

Chapter 8 Problem 8-2A or 8-2B *Name* ______________________________

Part 2 (Continued)

GENERAL JOURNAL

Date		Account Titles and Explanation	P. R.	Debit	Credit

Part 3

GENERAL JOURNAL

Date		Account Titles and Explanation	P. R.	Debit	Credit

Chapter 8 Problem 8-3A or 8-3B *Name* ____________________

2004:

GENERAL JOURNAL

Date		Account Titles and Explanation	P. R.	Debit	Credit

Supporting work:

2005:

GENERAL JOURNAL

Date		Account Titles and Explanation	P. R.	Debit	Credit

Supporting work:

Chapter 8 Problem 8-4A or 8-4B *Name* ______________________________

2004:

GENERAL JOURNAL

Date		Account Titles and Explanation	P. R.	Debit	Credit

2005:

GENERAL JOURNAL

Date		Account Titles and Explanation	P. R.	Debit	Credit

Supporting work:

 Name ____________________

2006:

GENERAL JOURNAL

Date		Account Titles and Explanation	P. R.	Debit	Credit

Supporting work:

Chapter 8 Problem 8-5A or 8-5B *Name* ______________________

Part 1

Year	Straight-Line	Units-of-Production	Double-Declining-Balance
1			
2			
3			
4			
5 (for 8-5B)			
Totals			

Workspace:

Straight-Line:

Units-of-Production:

Double-Declining-Balance:

Part 2

(a)

GENERAL JOURNAL

Date		Account Titles and Explanation	P. R.	Debit	Credit

(b)

GENERAL JOURNAL

Date		Account Titles and Explanation	P. R.	Debit	Credit

(c)

GENERAL JOURNAL

Date		Account Titles and Explanation	P. R.	Debit	Credit
(i) Sold for $ __________ cash:					
(ii) Sold for $ __________ cash:					
(iii) Destroyed in fire, collected $__________ cash from insurance.					

Chapter 8 Problem 8-6A or 8-6B *Name* ______________________
Part 1

GENERAL JOURNAL

Date		Account Titles and Explanation	P. R.	Debit	Credit
(a)					
(b)					
(c)					
(d)					
(e)					
(f)					

GENERAL JOURNAL

Date		Account Titles and Explanation	P. R.	Debit	Credit

Analysis Component:

Chapter 8 Problem 8-7A or 8-7B *Name* ____________________

Part 1

Part 2

Part 3

Part 4

Chapter 8 Serial Problem *Name* ______________________

Success Systems

(1)

(2)	December 31, 2004	December 31, 2005
Office Equipment:		
Computer Equipment:		

(3) Total Asset Turnover:

Analysis:

 Name ____________________

BTN 8-1

(1) As of Feb. 2, 2003:

As of Feb. 3, 2002

(2)

(3)

(4) Total Asset Turnover (2003):

Total Asset Turnover (2002):

(5) Roll On:

 Name ____________________

BTN 10-2

(1) Total Asset Turnover (Krispy Kreme):

Current Year

One Year Prior

Total Asset Turnover (Tastykake):

Current Year

One Year Prior

(2) Efficiency Analysis:

Chapter 8 Ethics Challenge--BTN 8-3 *Name* ____________________

(1)

(2)

(3)

Name ______________________________

DATA FOR MEMORANDUM

Total Asset Turnover	Company 1	Company 2	Company 3	Company 4	Company 5	Average

MEMORANDUM

TO:

FROM:

SUBJECT:

DATE:

Chapter 8 Taking It to the Net ***Name*** ______________________

BTN 8-5

(1)

(2)

(3)

Chapter 8 Teamwork in Action *Name* ____________________

BTN 10-6

Presentation Outline

Method of Expertise:

Depreciation Expense:

Explanations:

Analysis Versus Other Methods:

Book Value and Reporting:

Chapter 8 *Business Week* Name

Activity--BTN 8-7

(1)

(2)

(3)

(4)

Chapter 8 Entrepreneurial Decision--BTN 8-8 Name ____________________

Part 1

(a) ____________________

(b) ____________________

Part 2

Global Decision--BTN 8-10

(1) Total Asset Turnover (Current Year):

Total Asset Turnover (Prior Year):

(2)

Chapter 9 Quick Study 9-1 *Name* ______________________

Current Liabilities:

____

____

____

Quick Study 9-2

GENERAL JOURNAL

Date		Account Titles and Explanation	P. R.	Debit	Credit

Quick Study 9-3

GENERAL JOURNAL

Date		Account Titles and Explanation	P. R.	Debit	Credit

Chapter 9 Quick Study 9-4 *Name* ______________________

(1) Accrued Interest Payable:

(2) & (3)

GENERAL JOURNAL

Date		Account Titles and Explanation	P. R.	Debit	Credit

Quick Study 9-5

GENERAL JOURNAL

Date		Account Titles and Explanation	P. R.	Debit	Credit

Quick Study 9-6

GENERAL JOURNAL

Date		Account Titles and Explanation	P. R.	Debit	Credit

 Quick Study 9-7 *Name* ______________________

GENERAL JOURNAL

Date		Account Titles and Explanation	P. R.	Debit	Credit

Quick Study 9-8

(1) ______________________

(2) ______________________

(3) ______________________

Quick Study 9-9

Times Interest Earned: ______________________

Interpretation: ______________________

Quick Study 9-10[B]

GENERAL JOURNAL

Date		Account Titles and Explanation	P. R.	Debit	Credit

Chapter 9 Exercise 9-1 *Name* ______________________

(1)	(6)
(2)	(7)
(3)	(8)
(4)	(9)
(5)	(10)

Exercise 9-2

GENERAL JOURNAL

Date		Account Titles and Explanation	P. R.	Debit	Credit
(1)					
(2)					
(3)					
(4)					
(5)					
(6)					

Chapter 9 Exercise 9-3 (Continued) *Name* ______________________

1. ______________________

____

____

____

2.

GENERAL JOURNAL

Date		Account Titles and Explanation	P. R.	Debit	Credit

3.

GENERAL JOURNAL

Date		Account Titles and Explanation	P. R.	Debit	Credit

Chapter 9 Exercise 9-4 *Name* ______________________________

(1) Maturity Date: ______________________________

(2)

GENERAL JOURNAL

Date		Account Titles and Explanation	P. R.	Debit	Credit

 Name ______________________

(1) Maturity Date:

(2) Interest Expense (2005):

(3) Interest Expense (2006):

(4)

GENERAL JOURNAL

Date		Account Titles and Explanation	P. R.	Debit	Credit

 Name ______________________________

	Subject to Tax	Rate	Tax
(a)			
FICA-Social Security..........	________	________	________
FICA-Medicare.................	________	________	________
FUTA..............................	________	________	________
SUTA..............................	________	________	________
(b)			
FICA-Social Security..........	________	________	________
FICA-Medicare.................	________	________	________
FUTA..............................	________	________	________
SUTA..............................	________	________	________
(c)			
FICA-Social Security..........	________	________	________
FICA-Medicare.................	________	________	________
FUTA..............................	________	________	________
SUTA..............................	________	________	________

 Name ______________________

GENERAL JOURNAL

Date		Account Titles and Explanation	P. R.	Debit	Credit

Exercise 9-8

(1)

(2)

(3)

(4)

(5)

GENERAL JOURNAL

Date		Account Titles and Explanation	P. R.	Debit	Credit

Exercise 9-9

(a) ______________________________

(b) ______________________________

(c) ______________________________

(d) ______________________________

(e) ______________________________

(f) ______________________________

Analysis: ______________________________

Chapter 9 Exercise 9-10[A] *Name* ____________________

Exercise 9-11[A]

Exercise 9-12[B]

(1)

(2)

GENERAL JOURNAL

Date		Account Titles and Explanation	P. R.	Debit	Credit

Chapter 9 Problem 9-1A or 9-1B *Name* ______________________

(1) Maturity Dates:

(2) Interest Due at Maturity:

(3) Accrued Interest at the End of 2004:

(4) Interest Expense in 2005:

Chapter 9 Problem 9-1A or 9-1B (Continued) *Name* ______________________________

(5)

GENERAL JOURNAL

Date		Account Titles and Explanation	P. R.	Debit	Credit

(1)

GENERAL JOURNAL

Date		Account Titles and Explanation	P. R.	Debit	Credit
2004					

(1) (Continued from prior page)

GENERAL JOURNAL

Date		Account Titles and Explanation	P. R.	Debit	Credit
2005					

(2) Warranty Expense for November 2004 and December 2004:

(3) Warranty Expense for January 2005:

(4) Balance of the Estimated Warranty Liability as of December 31, 2004:

(5) Balance of the Estimated Warranty Liability as of December 31, 2005:

Chapter 9 Exercise 9-3A or 9-3B *Name* ______________________

(1) ____________ Company:

Times Interest Earned:

(2) ____________ Company:

Times Interest Earned:

(3) Sales Increase by ______ %

	____________ Company	____________ Company
Sales		
Variable expenses		
Income before interest		
Interest expense (fixed)		
Net Income		
Net income percent change		

(4) Sales Increase by ______ %

	____________ Company	____________ Company
Sales		
Variable expenses		
Income before interest		
Interest expense (fixed)		
Net Income		
Net income percent change		

 Name ______________________

(5) Sales Increase by ______ %

	________ Company	________ Company
Sales		
Variable expenses		
Income before interest		
Interest expense (fixed)		
Net Income		
Net income percent change		

(6) Sales Decrease by ______ %

	________ Company	________ Company
Sales		
Variable expenses		
Income before interest		
Interest expense (fixed)		
Net Income		
Net income percent change		

(7) Sales Decrease by ______ %

	________ Company	________ Company
Sales		
Variable expenses		
Income before interest		
Interest expense (fixed)		
Net Income		
Net income percent change		

 Name ____________________

(8) Sales Decrease by ______ %

	________ Company	________ Company
Sales		
Variable expenses		
Income before interest		
Interest expense (fixed)		
Net Income		
Net income percent change		

(9) Analysis:

Chapter 9 Exercise 9-4A or 9-4B *Name* ______________________

(1) Each Employee's FICA Withholdings for Social Security:

	Dale or Alli	Ted or Eve	Kate or Hong	Chas or Juan	Total
Maximum base					
Earned through ________					
Amt. subject to tax					
Earned this week					
Subject to tax					
Tax rate					
Social Security tax					

(2) Each Employee's FICA Withholdings for Medicare:

	Dale or Alli	Ted or Eve	Kate or Hong	Chas or Juan	Total
Earned this week					
Tax rate					
Medicare tax					

(3) Employer's FICA Taxes for Social Security:

	Dale or Alli	Ted or Eve	Kate or Hong	Chas or Juan	Total

(4) Employer's FICA Taxes for Medicare:

	Dale or Alli	Ted or Eve	Kate or Hong	Chas or Juan	Total

Chapter 9 Exercise 9-4A or 9-4B (Continued) *Name* ____________________

(5) Employer's FUTA Taxes:

	Dale or Alli	Ted or Eve	Kate or Hong	Chas or Juan	Total
Maximum base					
Earned through ________					
Amt. subject to tax					
Earned this week					
Subject to tax					
Tax rate					
FUTA rate					

(6) Employer's SUTA Taxes:

	Dale or Alli	Ted or Eve	Kate or Hong	Chas or Juan	Total
Subject to tax					
Tax rate					
SUTA tax					

(7) Each Employee's Take-Home Pay:

	Dale or Alli	Ted or Eve	Kate or Hong	Chas or Juan	Total
Gross earnings					
Less:					
FICA Soc. Sec. tax					
FICA Medicare tax					
Withholding taxes					
Health Insurance					
Take-home pay					

(8) Employer's Total Payroll-Related Expense for Each Employee:

	Dale or Alli	Ted or Eve	Kate or Hong	Chas or Juan	Total
Gross earnings					
Plus:					
FICA Soc. Sec. tax					
FICA Medicare tax					
FUTA tax					
SUTA tax					
Health Insurance					
Pension contrib.					
Total payroll exp.					

Chapter 9 Exercise 9-5A or 9-5B *Name* ______________________________

(1)

GENERAL JOURNAL

Date		Account Titles and Explanation	P. R.	Debit	Credit

(2)

GENERAL JOURNAL

Date		Account Titles and Explanation	P. R.	Debit	Credit

 Name ______________________

GENERAL JOURNAL

Date		Account Titles and Explanation	P. R.	Debit	Credit

Work Space:

Name ______________________________

GENERAL JOURNAL

Date		Account Titles and Explanation	P. R.	Debit	Credit
Continued from prior page					

Work Space:

Chapter 9 Serial Problem *Name* ______________________
Success Systems

(1) ______________________

GENERAL JOURNAL

Date		Account Titles and Explanation	P. R.	Debit	Credit
(2)					
(3)					
(4)					

Work Space:

Chapter 9 Comprehensive Problem **Name** ______________________

Part 1 Bug-Off Exterminators

(a) Correct Ending Balance of Cash and the Amount of the Omitted Check:

(b) Allowance for Doubtful Accounts:

(c) Depreciation Expense on the Truck:

(d) Depreciation Expense on the Equipment:

 Name ______________________

(e) Adjusted Services Revenue and Unearned Services Revenue Balances:

(f) Warranty Expense and Estimated Warranty Liability:

(g) Interest Payable and Interest Expense:

Name ______________________

BUG-OFF EXTERMINATORS
December 31, 2005

Account Titles	Unadjusted Trial Balance		Adjustments		Adjusted Trial Balance	
	Dr.	Cr.	Dr.	Cr.	Dr.	Cr.
Cash						
Accounts Receivable						
Allowance for Doubtful Accounts						
Merchandise Inventory						
Trucks						
Accumulated Depreciation-Trucks						
Equipment						
Accum. Depreciation-Equipment						
Accounts Payable						
Estimated Warranty Liability						
Unearned Services Revenue						
Long-Term Notes Payable						
Interest Payable						
Common Stock						
Retained Earnings						
Dividends						
Extermination Services Revenue						
Interest Revenue						
Sales						
Cost of Goods Sold						
Depreciation Expense-Trucks						
Depreciation Expense-Equipment						
Wages Expense						
Interest Expense						
Rent Expense						
Bad Debts Expense						
Miscellaneous Expense						
Repairs Expense						
Utilities Expense						
Warranty Expense						
Totals						

Name ______________________

GENERAL JOURNAL

Date		Account Titles and Explanation	P. R.	Debit	Credit

Name ____________________

BUG-OFF EXTERMINATORS
Income Statement
For Year Ended December 31, 2005

BUG-OFF EXTERMINATORS
Statement of Retained Earnings
For Year Ended December 31, 2005

 Name ______________________

BUG-OFF EXTERMINATORS
Balance Sheet
December 31, 2005

Chapter 9 Reporting in Action *Name* ______________________

BTN 9-1

(1) Times Interest Earned (2003):

Times Interest Earned (2002):

Times Interest Earned (2001):

Interpretation:

(2)

(3) Roll On:

Chapter 9 Comparative Analysis *Name* ______________________________

BTN 9-2

(1) Krispy Kreme's Times Interest Earned (Current Year):

Krispy Kreme's Times Interest Earned (One Year Prior):

Krispy Kreme's Times Interest Earned (Two Years Prior):

Tastykake's Times Interest Earned (Current Year):

Tastykake's Times Interest Earned (One Year Prior):

Tastykake's Times Interest Earned (Two Years Prior):

(2) Interpretation:

Chapter 9 Ethics Challenge Name ____________________

BTN 9-3

(1)

(2)

Name ______________________________

MEMORANDUM

TO:
FROM:
SUBJECT:
DATE:

Chapter 9 Taking It to the Net *Name* ______________________

BTN 9-5

(1)

(2)

(3)

Teamwork in Action--BTN 9-6

(1)

 Name ____________________

(2)

GENERAL JOURNAL

Date		Account Titles and Explanation	P. R.	Debit	Credit

(3) Team Discussion

(4)

GENERAL JOURNAL

Date		Account Titles and Explanation	P. R.	Debit	Credit

(5) Team Discussion

Chapter 9 *Business Week* Activity *Name* ______________________

BTN 9-7

(1) ______________________

(2) ______________________

(3) ______________________

Chapter 9 Entrepreneurial Decision *Name* ______________________

Part 1 BTN 9-8

Times Interest Earned:

Part 2

Income Statement	
	Make Investment
Sales	
Depreciation	
Variable expenses	
Income before interest	
Interest expense	
Net income	
Times Interest Earned:	

Part 3

Income Statement		
	No Investment	Make Investment
Sales		
Depreciation		
Variable expenses		
Income before interest		
Interest expense		
Net income		
Times Interest Earned:		

Income Statement	No Investment	Make Investment
Sales		
Depreciation		
Variable expenses		
Income before interest		
Interest expense		
Net income		
Times Interest Earned:		

Part 5

Income Statement	No Investment	Make Investment
Sales		
Depreciation		
Variable expenses		
Income before interest		
Interest expense		
Net income		
Times Interest Earned:		

Part 6

Chapter 9 Hitting the Road   *Name* ______________________

BTN 9-9

Global Decision--BTN 9-10

(1) Times Interest Earned	Current Year	One Year Prior

(2)

Chapter 10 Quick Study 10-1 *Name* ______________________________

1.	________	Debenture	5.	________	Sinking fund bond
2	________	Bond indenture	6.	________	Convertible bond
3.	________	Bearer bond	7.	________	Secured bond
4.	________	Registered bond	8.	________	Serial bond

Quick Study 10-2

(1) Cash Proceeds:

(2) Total Bond Interest Expense:

(3) Bond Interest Expense on 1st Payment Date:

Quick Study 10-3

(1) Cash Proceeds:

(2) Total Bond Interest Expense:

(3) Bond Interest Expense on 1st Payment Date:

 Quick Study 10-4 *Name* ______________________________

GENERAL JOURNAL

Date		Account Titles and Explanation	P. R.	Debit	Credit

Quick Study 10-5

(a)

(b)

 Quick Study 10-6 *Name* ____________________

GENERAL JOURNAL

Date		Account Titles and Explanation	P. R.	Debit	Credit

Quick Study 10-7

GENERAL JOURNAL

Date		Account Titles and Explanation	P. R.	Debit	Credit

Quick Study 10-8

GENERAL JOURNAL

Date		Account Titles and Explanation	P. R.	Debit	Credit

 Name ______________________

(a)

(b)

(c)

Quick Study 10-10

Quick Study 10-11

Ratio Computations:

Analysis and Interpretation:

GENERAL JOURNAL

Date		Account Titles and Explanation	P. R.	Debit	Credit

Quick Study 10-13[c]

GENERAL JOURNAL

Date		Account Titles and Explanation	P. R.	Debit	Credit

 Name ______________________

(1)

____

____

____

____

(2)

GENERAL JOURNAL

	Date		Account Titles and Explanation	P. R.	Debit	Credit
(a)						
(b)						
(c)						

(3)

GENERAL JOURNAL

	Date		Account Titles and Explanation	P. R.	Debit	Credit
(a)						
(b)						

Chapter 10 Exercise 10-2 *Name* ______________________________

(1) ______________________________

(2) Total Bond Interest Expense:

(3)

Semiannual Period-End	Unamortized Discount	Carrying Value
1/01/2005		
6/30/2005		
12/31/2005		
6/30/2006		
12/31/2006		
6/30/2007		
12/31/2007		

Chapter 10 Exercise 10-3B *Name* ______________________

(1)

(2) Total Bond Interest Expense:

(3)

Semiannual Interest Period-End	(A) Cash Interest Paid (4.5% x $250,000)	(B) Bond Interest Expense [6% x Prior (E)]	(C) Discount Amortization [(B) - (A)]	(D) Unamortized Discount [Prior (D) - (C)]	(E) Carrying Value [$250,000-(D)]
1/01/2005					
6/30/2005					
12/31/2005					
6/30/2006					
12/31/2006					
6/30/2007					
12/31/2007					

 Name ______________________________

(1) ______________________________

____

____

____

(2) Total Bond Interest Expense: ______________________________

____

____

____

____

____

____

____

____

(3)

Semiannual Period-End	Unamortized Premium	Carrying Value
1/01/2005		
6/30/2005		
12/31/2005		
6/30/2006		
12/31/2006		
6/30/2007		
12/31/2007		

Chapter 10 Exercise 10-5[B] *Name* ____________________

(1)

(2) Total Bond Interest Expense:

(3)

Semiannual Interest Period-End	(A) Cash Interest Paid [6.5% x $800,000]	(B) Bond Interest Expense [6% x Prior (E)]	(C) Premium Amortization [(A) - (B)]	(D) Unamortized Premium [Prior (D) - (C)]	(E) Carrying Value [$800,000+(D)]
1/01/2005					
6/30/2005					
12/31/2005					
6/30/2006					
12/31/2006					
6/30/2007					
12/31/2007					

Chapter 10 Exercise 10-6 *Name* ____________________

(1) Semiannual Cash Interest Payment:

(2) Number of Payments:

(3)

(4) Market Price Computation:

(5)

GENERAL JOURNAL

Date		Account Titles and Explanation	P. R.	Debit	Credit

Chapter 10 Exercise 10-7 *Name* ______________________________

(1) Semiannual Cash Interest Payment:

(2) Number of Payments:

(3)

(4) Market Price Computation:

(5)

GENERAL JOURNAL

Date		Account Titles and Explanation	P. R.	Debit	Credit

 Name ______________________

(1) Cash proceeds from sale:

(2) Discount at issuance:

(3) Amortization for First 6 Years:

(4) Carrying value of the bonds at 12/31/2009:

(5) Purchase price:

(6) Loss on retirement:

(7)

GENERAL JOURNAL

Date		Account Titles and Explanation	P. R.	Debit	Credit

Exercise 10-9

(1)

(2)

GENERAL JOURNAL

Date		Account Titles and Explanation	P. R.	Debit	Credit

 Name ______________________________

(1)

Semiannual Period-End	Unamortized Discount	Carrying Value
6/01/2004		
11/30/2004		
5/31/2005		
11/30/2005		
5/31/2006		
11/30/2006		
5/31/2007		
11/30/2007		
5/31/2008		

Supporting computations:

 Name ______________________

(2)

GENERAL JOURNAL

Date		Account Titles and Explanation	P. R.	Debit	Credit

 Name ______________________

(1) Principal Amount in Each Payment:

(2)

Period Ending Date	(A) Beginning Balance [Prior (E)]	Payments (B) Debit Interest Expense + [7% x (A)]	(C) Debit Notes Payable = [$25,000/4]	(D) Credit Cash [(B) + (C)]	(E) Ending Balance [(A) - (C)]
2005					
2006					
2007					
2008					

 Name ______________________

GENERAL JOURNAL

Date		Account Titles and Explanation	P. R.	Debit	Credit

Chapter 10 Exercise 10-13 *Name* ______________________

(1) Amount of Each Payment:

(2)

Period Ending Date	(A) Beginning Balance [Prior (E)]	Payments: (B) Debit Interest Expense [7% x (A)]	+	Payments: (C) Debit Notes Payable [(D) - (B)]	=	Payments: (D) Credit Cash [computed]	(E) Ending Balance [(A) - (C)]
2005							
2006							
2007							
2008							

 Name ______________________

GENERAL JOURNAL

Date		Account Titles and Explanation	P. R.	Debit	Credit

 Name ______________________________

Chapter 10 Exercise 10-16[C] *Name* ______________________________

(1) ______________________________
(2) ______________________________
(3) ______________________________

Exercise 10-17[C]

GENERAL JOURNAL

Date		Account Titles and Explanation	P. R.	Debit	Credit
(1)					
(2)					

Exercise 10-18[C]

Part 1

(a)

	Cash Flow	PV Table	PV Table Value	Amount	Present Value

(b)

GENERAL JOURNAL

Date		Account Titles and Explanation	P. R.	Debit	Credit

Part 2

(a)

	Cash Flow	PV Table	PV Table Value	Amount	Present Value

(b)

GENERAL JOURNAL

Date		Account Titles and Explanation	P. R.	Debit	Credit

Chapter 10 Problem 10-1A or 10-1B *Name* ______________________

Part 3 (Continued)

(a)

Cash Flow	PV Table	PV Table Value	Amount	Present Value

(b)

GENERAL JOURNAL

Date		Account Titles and Explanation	P. R.	Debit	Credit

Problem 10-2A or 10-2B

Part 1

GENERAL JOURNAL

Date		Account Titles and Explanation	P. R.	Debit	Credit

(a) Cash Payment:

(b) Semiannual Amortization:

(c) Bond Interest Expense:

Part 3

Total Bond Interest Expense:

Part 4

Semiannual Period-End	Unamortized Discount	Carrying Value
1/01/2004		
6/30/2004		
12/31/2004		
6/30/2005		
12/31/2005		

GENERAL JOURNAL

Date		Account Titles and Explanation	P. R.	Debit	Credit

Part 6--Requirements 1 through 5 are repeated assuming a bond premium

Requirement 1

GENERAL JOURNAL

Date		Account Titles and Explanation	P. R.	Debit	Credit

Requirement 2

(a) Cash Payment:

(b) Semiannual Amortization:

(c) Bond Interest Expense:

Chapter 10 Problem 10-2A or 10-2B *Name* ______________________
Part 6 (Continued)

Requirement 3

Total Bond Interest Expense:

Requirement 4

Semiannual Period-End	Unamortized Premium	Carrying Value
1/01/2004		
6/30/2004		
12/31/2004		
6/30/2005		
12/31/2005		

Requirement 5

GENERAL JOURNAL

Date		Account Titles and Explanation	P. R.	Debit	Credit

Chapter 10 Problem 10-3A or 10-3B *Name* ______________________

Part 1

Total Bond Interest Expense:

Part 2

Semiannual Interest Period-End	Unamortized Premium	Carrying Value
1/01/2004		
6/30/2004		
12/31/2004		
6/30/2005		
12/31/2005		
6/30/2006		
12/31/2006		
6/30/2007		
12/31/2007		
6/30/2008		
12/31/2008		

GENERAL JOURNAL

Date		Account Titles and Explanation	P. R.	Debit	Credit

Chapter 10 Problem 10-4A[B] or 10-4B[B] *Name* ____________________

Part 1

Total Bond Interest Expense:

Part 2

Semiannual Interest Period-End	(A) Cash Interest Paid [__% x $____]	(B) Bond Interest Expense [__% x Prior (E)]	(C) Premium Amortization [(A) - (B)]	(D) Unamortized Premium [Prior (D) - (C)]	(E) Carrying Value [$____ + (D)]
1/01/2004					
6/30/2004					
12/31/2004					
6/30/2005					
12/31/2005					
6/30/2006					
12/31/2006					
6/30/2007					
12/31/2007					
6/30/2008					
12/31/2008					

Chapter 10 Problem 10-4A^{B} or 10-4B^{B} *Name* ______________________
Part 3 (Continued)

GENERAL JOURNAL

Date		Account Titles and Explanation	P. R.	Debit	Credit

Part 4

	Cash Flow	PV Table	PV Table Value	Amount	Present Value

Comparison to Part 2 Table:

Chapter 10 Problem 10-5A or 10-5B *Name* ______________________

Part 1

GENERAL JOURNAL

Date		Account Titles and Explanation	P. R.	Debit	Credit

Part 2

Total Bond Interest Expense:

Part 3

Semiannual Interest Period-End	Unamortized Discount	Carrying Value
1/01/2004		
6/30/2004		
12/31/2004		
6/30/2005		
12/31/2005		

Chapter 10 Problem 10-5A or 10-5B *Name* ______________________________

Part 4

GENERAL JOURNAL

Date		Account Titles and Explanation	P. R.	Debit	Credit

Part 5 (for Problem 10-5A only)

Chapter 10 Problem 10-6A[B] or 10-6B[B] *Name* ______________________

Part 1

GENERAL JOURNAL

Date		Account Titles and Explanation	P. R.	Debit	Credit

Part 2

Total Bond Interest Expense:

Part 3

Semiannual Interest Period-End	(A) Cash Interest Paid [__% x $___]	(B) Bond Interest Expense [__% x Prior (E)]	(C) Discount Amortization [(B) - (A)]	(D) Unamortized Discount [Prior (D) - (C)]	(E) Carrying Value [$____ - (D)]
1/01/2004					
6/30/2004					
12/31/2004					
6/30/2005					
12/31/2005					

Chapter 10 Problem 10-6A[B] or 10-6B[B] *Name* ____________________

Part 4

GENERAL JOURNAL

Date		Account Titles and Explanation	P. R.	Debit	Credit

Chapter 10 Problem 10-7A[B] or 10-7B[B] *Name* ______________________

Part 1

GENERAL JOURNAL

Date		Account Titles and Explanation	P. R.	Debit	Credit

Part 2

Total Bond Interest Expense:

Part 3

Semiannual Interest Period-End	(A) Cash Interest Paid [__% x $___]	(B) Bond Interest Expense [__% x Prior (E)]	(C) Discount Amortization [(A) - (B)]	(D) Unamortized Premium [Prior (D) - (C)]	(E) Carrying Value [$____ + (D)]
1/01/2004					
6/30/2004					
12/31/2004					
6/30/2005					
12/31/2005					

Part 4

GENERAL JOURNAL

Date		Account Titles and Explanation	P. R.	Debit	Credit

Part 5

GENERAL JOURNAL

Date		Account Titles and Explanation	P. R.	Debit	Credit

Part 6

Chapter 10 Problem 10-8A or 10-8B *Name* ______________________________

Part 1

Amount of Each Payment:

Part 2

			Payments		
	(A)	(B)	(C)	(D)	(E)
Period Ending Date	Beginning Balance [Prior (E)]	Debit Interest Expense + [___% x (A)]	Debit Notes Payable = [(D) - (B)]	Credit Cash [computed]	Ending Balance [(A) - (C)]

Chapter 10 Problem 10-8A or 10-8B *Name* ______________________
Part 3 (Continued)

GENERAL JOURNAL

Date		Account Titles and Explanation	P. R.	Debit	Credit

Part 4

Period Ending Date	*(A) Beginning Balance [Prior (E)]*	*(B) Debit Interest Expense [__% x (A)]*	+	*(C) Debit Notes Payable [$__/__yrs.]*	=	*(D) Credit Cash [(B) + (C)]*	*(E) Ending Balance [(A) - (C)]*

GENERAL JOURNAL

Date		Account Titles and Explanation	P. R.	Debit	Credit

Chapter 10 Problem 10-9A or 10-9B *Name* ____________________
Part 1

______________ Company Ratio:

______________ Company Ratio:

Part 2

Analysis and Interpretation:

Chapter 10 Problem 10-10A or 10-10B *Name* ______________________________

Part 1

Present Value of the Lease Payments:

Part 2

GENERAL JOURNAL

Date		Account Titles and Explanation	P. R.	Debit	Credit

Part 3

Capital Lease Liability Payment (Amortization) Schedule:

Period Ending Date	Beginning Balance of Lease Liability	Interest on Lease Liability (__%)	Reduction of Lease Liability	Cash Lease Payment	Ending Balance of Lease Liability
Year 1					
Year 2					
Year 3					
Year 4					
Year 5					
Year 6					
Year 7					

Part 4

GENERAL JOURNAL

Date		Account Titles and Explanation	Ref.	Debit	Credit

Chapter 10 Serial Problem *Name* ______________________

Success Systems

Part 1

Maximum Loan Allowed:

Part 2

(a) Percent of Assets Financed by Debt

(b) Percent of Assets Financed by Equity

 Name ______________________________

BTN 10-1

(1) ____

(2) ____

(3) ____

(4) Roll On: ____

(1) Krispy Kreme

Current Year:

Prior Year:

Tastykake

Current Year:

Prior Year:

(2)

Chapter 10 Ethics Challenge Name ______________________________
BTN 10-3

(1) ______________________________

(2) ______________________________

MEMORANDUM

TO:
FROM:
DATE:
SUBJECT:

 Name ______________________________

(1) Debt Issued:

(2) Debt Repaid:

(3) Stock Issued:

(4)

 Name ________________

Parts 1 and 2 BTN 10-6

Part 3

Part 4

Similarities	Differences

Chapter 10 Business Week Activity *Name* ______________________

Part 1 BTN 10-7

Part 2

Part 3

Part 4

Part 5

Chapter 10 Entrepreneurial Decision *Name* ______________________________
Part 1 BTN 10-8

		Alternative Notes for Expansion				
	Current	10% Note	15% Note	16% Note	17% Note	20% Note
Income before interest............						
interest............						
Net income.......						
Equity...............						
Return on equity..						

Work Space:

Part 2

BTN 10-9

Name ______________________

Global Decision--BTN 10-10

(1) GP's Current Year Ratio:

GP's Prior Year Ratio:

(2)

(3)

Chapter 11 Quick Study 11-1 *Name* ____________________

True Statements:

Quick Study 11-2

GENERAL JOURNAL

Date		Account Titles and Explanation	P. R.	Debit	Credit

Quick Study 11-3

Cash Dividend to Common Shareholders

 Name ____________________

GENERAL JOURNAL

Date		Account Titles and Explanation	P. R.	Debit	Credit

Quick Study 11-5

Catalina Company
Stockholders' Equity
April 2 (after stock dividend)

 Quick Study 11-6 *Name* ______________________

GENERAL JOURNAL

Date		Account Titles and Explanation	P. R.	Debit	Credit

Quick Study 11-7

(1)

(2)

Quick Study 11-8

Basic Earnings Per Share

 Name ______________________

Time Period	Outstanding Shares	Fraction of Year	Weighted Average

Quick Study 11-10

Time Period	Outstanding Shares	Effect of Dividend	Fraction of Year	Weighted Average

Quick Study 11-11

 Quick Study 11-12 *Name* ______________________________

Dividend Yield

____

____

____

Analysis

____

____

____

Quick Study 11-13

Price-Earnings Ratio

____

____

____

Analysis

____

____

____

 Exercise 11-1 *Name* ______________________

	Characteristic	Corporations
1.	Owner authority & control	
2.	Ease of formation	
3.	Transferability of ownership	
4.	Ability to raise large amounts of capital	
5.	Duration of Life	
6.	Owner liability	
7.	Legal status	
8.	Tax status of income	

Exercise 11-2

GENERAL JOURNAL

Date		Account Titles and Explanation	P. R.	Debit	Credit
(1)					
(2)					
(3)					

GENERAL JOURNAL

Date		Account Titles and Explanation	P. R.	Debit	Credit
(1)					
(2)					
(3)					
(4)					

Exercise 11-4

(1) ______________________	(4) ______________________
(2) ______________________	(5) ______________________
(3) ______________________	(6) ______________________

 Exercise 11-5 *Name* ______________________

	Preferred	Common
2003:		
2004:		
2005:		
2006:		
Total:		

Exercise 11-6

	Preferred	Common
2003:		
2004:		
2005:		
2006:		
Total:		

 Name ______________________

Part 1

(a) Retained Earnings:

(b) Total Stockholders' Equity:

(c) Number of Outstanding Shares:

Part 2

(a) Retained Earnings:

(b) Total Stockholders' Equity:

(c) Number of Outstanding Shares:

Part 3

Chapter 11 Exercise 11-8 ***Name*** ______________________________

Part 1

GENERAL JOURNAL

Date		Account Titles and Explanation	P. R.	Debit	Credit

Part 2

	Before	After

Part 3

	Feb. 5	Feb. 28

Chapter 11 Exercise 11-9 *Name* ______________________

Part 1

GENERAL JOURNAL

Date		Account Titles and Explanation	P. R.	Debit	Credit

Changes to the equity section include:

Revised Stockholders' Equity Section (for support of your part 2 solution):

 Exercise 11-10 *Name* ______________________

(1)
(2)
(3)
(4)
(5)
(6)
(7)
(8)
(9)

Exercise 11-11

RANDA MERCHANDISING, INC.
Income Statement
For Year Ended December 31, 2005

Chapter 11 Exercise 11-12 *Name* ______________________

Part 1

Part 2

Chapter 11 Exercise 11-13 *Name* ______________________________

(1) Net Income Available to Common Stockholders:

(2)

Time Period	*Outstanding Shares*	*Fraction of Year*	*Weighted Average*

(3) Basic Earnings Per Share:

Chapter 11 Exercise 11-14 *Name* ______________________________

(1) Net Income Available to Common Stockholders:

(2)

Time Period	Original Shares	Effect of Split	Fraction of Year	Weighted Average

(3) Basic Earnings Per Share:

Exercise 11-15

(1)

(2) ______________________

Exercise 11-16
Dividend Yield:

(1) ______________________

(2) ______________________

(3) ______________________

(4) ______________________

Analysis: ______________________

Exercise 11-17
Price-Earnings Ratio:

(1) ______________________

(2) ______________________

(3) ______________________

(4) ______________________

Analysis: ______________________

Chapter 11 Problem 11-1A or 11-1B *Name* ____________________

Part 1

(a)

(b)

(c)

(d)

Part 2

Number of Outstanding Shares:

Part 3

Minimum Legal Capital:

Part 4

Total Contributed Capital from Common Stockholders:

Part 5

Book Value Per Common Share:

Chapter 11 Problem 11-2A or 11-2B *Name* ____________________

Part 1

GENERAL JOURNAL

Date		Account Titles and Explanation	P. R.	Debit	Credit

______________ CORPORATION
Statement of Retained Earnings
For Year Ended December 31, 2006

Part 3

______________ CORPORATION
Stockholders' Equity Section of the Balance Sheet
December 31, 2006

Chapter 11 Problem 11-3A or 11-3B *Name* ______________________

Part 1

Explanations for each of the entries:

Oct. 2 (Jan.17)* ______________________

____

Oct 25 (Feb. 5)* ______________________

____

Oct. 31 (Feb. 28)* ______________________

____

Nov. 5 (Mar. 14)* ______________________

____

Dec. 1(Mar. 25)* ______________________

____

Dec. 31 (Mar. 31)* ______________________

____

* Dates for Problem 11-3B are in parentheses.

Part 2

	Oct. 2 (Jan. 17)*	Oct. 25 (Feb. 5)*	Oct. 31 (Feb. 28)*	Nov. 5 (Mar. 14)*	Dec. 1 (Mar. 25)*	Dec. 31 (Mar. 31)*
Common stock..............						
Common stock dividend distributable...						
Contributed capital in excess of par............						
Retained earnings........						
Total equity.................						

*Dates for Problem 11-3B are in parentheses.

Problem 11-4A or 11-4B

Part 1

Outstanding Common Shares ______________________

____

____

____

____

____

____

____

Cash Dividend Amount:

Part 3

Capitalization of Retained Earnings:

Part 4

Cost Per Share of Treasury Stock:

Part 5

Net Income Computation:

 Name ______________________

Part 1 Effect of Income Taxes:

Items	Pre-Tax	___% Tax Effect	After-Tax

Part 2 Income from Continuing Operations:

Part 3 Income from Discontinued Segment:

Part 4 Income before Extraordinary Items and Cumulative Effect of Change in Principle:

Part 5 Net Income:

Problem 11-6A or 11-6B

Part 1

Part 2 Double-Declining-Balance Depreciation:

Year	Beginning-Year Book Value	Depreciation Expense	Year-End Book Value

 Name ______________________

Part 3 Straight-Line Depreciation:

Year	Beginning-Year Book Value	Depreciation Expense	Year-End Book Value

Part 4 Calculation of Cumulative Effect:

Part 5

Part 6

Chapter 11 Problem 11-6A or 11-6B (Continued) *Name* ______

Part 7 Effect of Error on Financial Statements:

Problem 11-7A or 11-7B

Part 1 2003 weighted-average shares:

Time Period	Outstanding Shares	Effect of Dividend	Fraction of Year	Weighted Average

Part 2 2003 earnings per share components:

	Reported Total	Divided by Shares	Earnings per Share

Chapter 11 Problem 11-7A or 11-7B (Continued) *Name* ______________________

Part 3 2004 weighted-average shares:

Time Period	Outstanding Shares	Fraction of Year	Weighted Average

Part 4 2004 earnings per share components:

	Reported Total	Divided by Shares	Earnings per Share

Part 5 2005 weighted-average shares:

Time Period	Outstanding Shares	Effect of Split	Fraction of Year	Weighted Average

Part 6 2005 earnings per share components:

	Reported Total	Divided by Shares	Earnings per Share

Problem 11-8A or 11-8B

(1) Market Price Per Share:

(2) Computation of Stock Par Values:

(3) Book Value Per Preferred Share:

Book Value Per Common Share:

(4) Book Value Per Preferred Share:

Book Value Per Common Share:

(5) Book Value Per Preferred Share:

Book Value Per Common Share:

(6)

(7)

 Name ____________________

BTN 11-1

(1)

(2)

(3)

(4)

(5)

(6)

(7)

(8) **Roll On:**

BTN 11-2

(1)

Krispy Kreme Book Value Per Common Share:

Tastykake Book Value Per Common Share:

(2)

Krispy Kreme Earnings Per Share:

Tastykake Earnings per Share:

(3)

Krispy Kreme Dividend Yield:

Tastykake Dividend Yield:

Analysis:

(4)

Krispy Kreme Price-Earnings Ratio:

Tastykake Price-Earnings Ratio:

Analysis & Interpretation:

Name

MEMORANDUM

TO:
FROM:
DATE:
SUBJECT:

Company	Earnings Per Share	Market Price of Stock	Price-Earnings Ratio

Industry Norm:

Meaning of Price-Earnings Ratio:

Comparison Across Companies:

Concluding Analysis:

Chapter 11 Taking It to the Net Name ______________________

Part 1 BTN 11-5

Part 2

Part 3

Part 4

Part 5

Name ______________________

Part 1

(a) Impact on Financial Position due to Stock Buyback:

(b) Reasons for Stock Buyback:

 Name ______________________

Part 2 BTN 11-6 (Continued)

GENERAL JOURNAL

Date		Account Titles and Explanation	P. R.	Debit	Credit
Reacquisition entry					
(a)					
(b)					
(c)					
(d)					
(e)					

Part 3

Similarities:

Differences:

Chapter 11 *Business Week* Activity **BTN 11-7** *Name* ____________________

(1) ____________________

(2) ____________________

(3) ____________________

(4) ____________________

(5) ____________________

 Name ____________________

Part 1 BTN 11-8

	Plan A	Plan B

Part 2

	Plan A	Plan B

Part 3

 Hitting the Road--BTN 11-9 *Name* ______________________________

Global Decision--BTN 11-10

(1) Earnings per share

(2) Weighted Average Shares Outstanding

(3) Cash Dividends Declared

Chapter 12 Quick Study 12-1 *Name* ____________________

(1)

(2)

(3)

(4)

Quick Study 12-2

(1)	(6)
(2)	(7)
(3)	(8)
(4)	(9)
(5)	(10)

Quick Study 12-3

Cash Flow from Operating Activities

Cash Inflow from Sale of Furniture:

Quick Study 12-5

(1) Cash Paid for Dividends

(1) Cash Payments toward Notes:

Quick Study 12-6[B]

(1) Cash Received from Customer Sales:

(2) Net Increase or Decrease in Cash:

Chapter 12 Quick Study 12-7[B] *Name* ______________________

(1) Cash Paid for Merchandise:

(2) Cash Paid for Operating Expenses:

Quick Study 12-8[B]

Cash Flow from Operating Activities

Quick Study 12-9

(1)

(2)

 Name ______________________

____
____
____
____
____
____
____
____

Exercise 12-1

Cash Flow from Operating Activities

 Name ____________________

	Statement of Cash Flows			Noncash Investing & Financing Activities	Not Reported on Statement or in Note
	Operating Activities	Investing Activities	Financing Activities		
a. Paid cash to purchase inventory.					
b. Purchased land by issuing stock.					
c. Accounts receivable decreased in the year.					
d. Sold equipment for cash, yielding a loss.					
e. Recorded depreciation expense.					
f. Income taxes payable increased in the year.					
g. Declared and paid a cash dividend.					

 Name ____________________

	Statement of Cash Flows			Noncash Investing & Financing Activities	Not Reported on Statement or in Note
	Operating Activities	Investing Activities	Financing Activities		
a. Retired long-term bonds payable by issuing stock.					
b. Depreciation expense recorded.					
c. Paid cash dividend that was declared in a prior period					
d. Sold inventory for cash.					
e. Borrowed cash from bank by signing a 9-month note payable.					
f. Paid cash to purchase patent.					
g. Six-month note receivable is accepted in exchange for plant assets.					

Chapter 12 Exercise 12-4[B] *Name* ______________________________

Case A

Case B

Case C

KANSAS COMPANY

Statement of Cash Flows

For Year Ended December 31, 2005

 Name ______________________________

Cash Flows from Operating Activities

Supporting computations:

Exercise 12-7[B]

Cash Flows from Operating Activities

Supporting computations:

 Name ______________________

Cash Flows from Operating Activities

 Name ______________________

Gecko, Inc.
Statement of Cash Flows (Indirect Method)
For Year Ended June 30, 2005

Supporting Computations:

(1) Cash received from sale of equipment:

Cash paid for new equipment:

(2) Cash paid to retire notes:

(3) Cash paid for dividends:

Part 2

Cash Flow on Total Assets Ratio:

Interpretation:

Gecko, Inc.
Statement of Cash Flows (Direct Method)
For Year Ended June 30, 2005

Supporting Computations:

(1) Cash received from customers:

(2) Cash paid for merchandise inventory:

(3) Cash paid for other operating expenses:

(4) Cash paid for income taxes:

(5) Cash received from sale of equipment:

Cash paid for new equipment:

(6) Cash paid to retire notes:

(7) Cash paid for dividends:

Part 2

Cash Flow on Total Assets:

Chapter 12 Exercise 12-11[B] *Name* ______________________________

Part 1

TEXAS CORPORATION

Statement of Cash Flows

For Year Ended December 31, 2005

Part 2

(a)

(b)

(c)

(d)

Chapter 12 Problem 12-1A or 12-1B *Name* ____________________

Part 1

Statement of Cash Flows

For Year Ended December 31, 2005

Supporting calculations:

Statement of Cash Flows
For Year Ended December 31, 2005

Supporting calculations:

Spreadsheet for Statement of Cash Flows
For Year Ended December 31, 2005

	Dec. 31, 2004	Analysis of changes: Debit	Analysis of changes: Credit	Dec. 31, 2005
Balance sheet-debits:				
Cash..				
Accounts receivable......................				
Merchandise inventory..................				
Prepaid expenses.........................				
Equipment....................................				
Balance sheet-credits:				
Accum. depreciation-Equip.......				
Accounts payable.....................				
Short-term notes payable.........				
Long-term notes payable..........				
Common Stock, $___par value...				
Contributed capital in excess of par value, common stock.......				
Retained earnings..................				
Statement of cash flows:				
Operating activities				
Net income..............................				
________ in accts. receivable...				
________ in merch. inventory...				
________ in prepaid expenses...				
________ in accounts payable...				
Depreciation expense..............				
________ on sale of equipment..				
Investing activities				
Receipt from sale of equipment...				
Payment to purchase equipment..				
Financing activities				
Borrowed on short-term note....				
Payment on long-term note......				
Issued common stock for cash..				
Payments of cash dividends.....				
Noncash investing and financing activities				
Purchase of equip. financed by long-term note payable.....				

 Name ____________________

Statement of Cash Flows
For Year Ended December 31, 2005

Supporting calculations:

 Name ______________________

Statement of Cash Flows
For Year Ended December 31, 2005

Supporting calculations:

 Name ______________________

Spreadsheet for Statement of Cash Flows
For Year Ended December 31, 2005

	Dec. 31, 2004	Analysis of changes Debit	Analysis of changes Credit	Dec. 31, 2005
Balance sheet-debits:				
Cash				
Accounts receivable				
Merchandise inventory				
Equipment				
Balance sheet-credits:				
Accum. depreciation-Equip				
Accounts payable				
Income taxes payable				
Common stock, $___par value				
Contributed capital in excess of par value, common stock				
Retained earnings				
Statement of cash flows:				
Operating activities				
Net income				
________ in accts. receivable				
________ in merch. inventory				
________ in accounts payable				
________ in income taxes payable				
Depreciation expense				
Investing activities				
Payment for equipment				
Financing activities				
Issued common stock for cash				
Paid cash dividends				

Chapter 12 Serial Problem *Name* ______________________
Success Systems

SUCCESS SYSTEMS
Statement of Cash Flows
For Three Months Ended March 31, 2005

Supporting calculations:

 Name ____________

BTN 12-1

(1)

(2)

(3)

(4)

(5) **Roll On:**

(1) Krispy Kreme's Cash Flow on Total Assets Ratio:

Current Year

Prior Year

Tastykake's Cash Flow on Total Assets Ratio:

Current Year

Prior Year

(2)

(3)

(4)

Chapter 12 Ethics Challenge BTN 12-3 *Name* ______________________________

(1) (a)

(b)

(2)

MEMORANDUM

TO:
FROM:
DATE:
SUBJECT:

 Name ____________

BTN 12-5

(1)

(2)

(3)	2003	2002	2001
Net income (net loss)			
Cash flow from operations			

Analysis:

(4)

(5)

(6)

Teamwork in Action--BTN 12-6

Part 1

(a)

(b) **Similarities** **Differences**

(c)

(d)

Part 2

Adjusting Net Income to Cash Flow from Operating Activities	
Items to Add	**Items to Subtract**

a.
b.
c.
d.

(a)

(b)

(c)

(d)

Name ______________________________

(1) ______________________________

(2) ______________________________

(3) ______________________________

(4) ______________________________

Chapter 12 Entrepreneurial Decision *Name* ______________________

BTN 12-8

(1) ______________________

(2) ______________________

(3) ______________________

Name ______________________

MEMORANDUM

TO:
FROM:
DATE:
SUBJECT:

 Name ______________________

BTN 12-10

(1) ______________________

(2) ______________________

(3) ______________________

Global Decision--BTN 12-11

(1) ______________________

(2) ______________________

(3) ______________________

(4) ______________________

 Name ______________________

Quick Study 13-2

Quick Study 13-3

	2005	2004	Dollar Change	Percent Change

Chapter 13 Quick Study 13-4 *Name* ______________________

(1) Common-Size Percents

2005

2004

(2) Trend Percents

2005

2004

Quick Study 13-5

(1) (6)

(2) (7)

(3) (8)

(4) (9)

(5) (10)

Quick Study 13-6

(1)

(2)

(3)

Quick Study 13-7

Ratio	2005	2004	Trend
1. Profit Margin Ratio	8%	6%	
2. Debt Ratio	45%	40%	
3. Gross Margin Ratio	33%	45%	
4. Acid-Test Ratio	0.99	1.10	
5. Accounts Receivable Turnover	5.4	6.6	
6. Basic Earnings Per Share	$1.24	$1.20	
7. Inventory Turnover	3.5	3.3	
8. Dividend Yield	1.0%	0.8%	

 Exercise 13-1 *Name* ______________________

	2007	2006	2005	2004	2003

Analysis:

Exercise 13-2

 Name ______________________

	2005	2004

Analysis:

COMPARATIVE ANALYSIS REPORT

 Name ______________________

COMPARATIVE ANALYSIS REPORT

Sexton Company
Common-Size Comparative Balance Sheets
December 31, 2004-2006

	2006	2005	2004

Analysis and interpretation:

Chapter 13 Exercise 13-7 *Name* ______________________________

(1) Current Ratio:

2006:

2005:

2004:

(2) Acid-test ratio

2006:

2005:

2004:

Analysis and interpretation:

 Name ______________________________

1. Days' sales uncollected:

2006:

2005:

2. Accounts receivable turnover:

2006:

2005:

3. Inventory turnover:

2006:

2005:

4. Days' sales in inventory:

2006:

2005:

Analysis and interpretation:

 Name ____________________

(1)

(2)

(3)

Analysis and interpretation:

(1) Profit margin:

2006:

2005:

(2) Total asset turnover:

2006:

2005:

(3) Return on total assets:

2006:

2005:

Analysis and interpretation:

 Name ______________________________

(1) Return on common stockholders' equity:

2006:

2005:

(2) Price-earnings ratio, December 31:

2006:

2005:

(3) Dividend yield:

2006:

2005:

Analysis and interpretation:

Chapter 13 Problem 13-1A or 13-1B *Nam*e ____________________

Part 1

2006:

2005:

2004:

Part 2

Common-Size Comparative Income Statements For Years Ended December 31, 2006, 2005, and 2004	2006	2005	2004

Balance Sheet Data in Trend Percents December 31, 2006, 2005, and 2004	2006	2005	2004

Part 4

Significant relations revealed:

 Name ______________________

Income Statement Trends For Years Ended December 31, 2006-2000	2006	2005	2004	2003	2002	2001	2000

Balance Sheet Trends December 31, 2006-2000	2006	2005	2004	2003	2002	2001	2000

Analysis and interpretation:

 Name ______________________

Transaction	*Current Assets*	*Quick Assets*	*Current Liabilities*	*Current Ratio*	*Acid-Test Ratio*	*Working Capital*
Beg. Bal.						

Supporting computations:

 Name ____________________

(1) Current ratio:

(2) Acid-test ratio:

(3) Days' sales uncollected:

(4) Inventory turnover:

(5) Days' sales in inventory:

(6) Ratio of pledged assets to secured liabilities:

(7) Times interest earned:

(8) Profit margin ratio:

(9) Total asset turnover:

(10) Return on total assets:

(11) Return on common stockholders' equity:

 Name ______________________

Part 1

	Company		Company

a. Current ratio:

b. Acid-test ratio:

c. Accounts (incl. notes) receivable turnover:

d. Inventory turnover:

e. Days' sales in inventory:

f. Days' sales uncollected:

Short-term credit risk analysis:

Part 2

	______ Company	______ Company
a. Profit margin ratio:		
b. Total asset turnover:		
c. Return on total assets:		
d. Return on common stockholders' equity:		
e. Price-earnings ratio:		
f. Dividend yield:		

Investment analysis:

Name ______________________________

(1) Gross Margin Ratio (with services revenue):

Gross Margin Ratio (without services revenue):

Profit Margin Ratio:

(2) Current Ratio:

Acid-Test Ratio:

(3) Debt Ratio:

Equity Ratio:

(4) Current Assets as % of Total Assets:

Long-Term Assets as % of Total Assets:

BTN 13-1

Name ______________________________

(1) Trend Percents for selected income statement accounts:

	2003	2002	2001
Revenues			
Cost of sales (Operating expenses)			
General and administrative expenses			
Income taxes			
Net income			

(2) Common-size percents for asset categories and accounts:

	2003	2002
Total current assets		
Property and equipment, net		
Intangible assets		
Accrued expenses		

(3) Analysis and Interpretation:

(4) Roll On

 Name ______________________

(1)

Key figures	Krispy Kreme	Tastykake
Cash and cash equivalents		
Accounts receivable, net		
Inventories		
Retained earnings		
Cost of sales*		
Revenues (and Sales)		
Total Assets		

* Krispy Kreme's cost of sales is titled operating expenses.

(2)

(3)

(4)

Chapter 13 Ethics Challenge BTN 13-3 *Name* ____________________

(1)

(2)

MEMORANDUM

TO:
FROM:
DATE:
SUBJECT:

 Name ______________________

BTN 13-5

	2002	2001
1. Profit margin ratio		
2. Gross profit ratio		
3. Return on total assets		
4. Return on common stockholders' equity		
5. Basic earnings per share		

Analysis and Interpretation:

Chapter 13 Teamwork in Action *Name* ____________________

BTN 13-6

Part 1

Part 2

Part 3

Chapter 13 *Business Week Activity* **Name** ______________________

BTN 13-7

(1)

(2)

(3)

(4)

(5)

Chapter 13 Entrepreneurial Decision *Name* ______________________

BTN 13-8

(1)

(2)

(3)

(4)

(5)

(6)

Hitting the Road--BTN 13-9

 Name ______________________________

Identification of Differences:

(1) ______________________________

____

(2) ______________________________

____

(3) ______________________________

____

(4) ______________________________

____

(5) ______________________________

____

Appendix B Quick Study B-1 *Name* ______________________

(1) ______________________

(2) ______________________

(3) ______________________

(4) ______________________

Quick Study B-2

Annual Rate of Interest

Quick Study B-3

Years of Investment

Quick Study B-4

Value of Investment

Quick Study B-5

Cash Proceeds at Liquidation

Quick Study B-6

Amount Willing to Pay for Project

 Name ______________________

Future Value of Retirement Program

Exercise B-1

Years Until Payment

Exercise B-2

Rate of Interest to be Earned

Exercise B-3

Rate of Interest to be Earned

Exercise B-4

Number of Annual Payments to be Received

Exercise B-5

Rate of Interest to be Earned

 Exercise B-6 *Name* ______________________

Number of Annual Investments

Exercise B-7

Cost (Present Value) of Automobile

Exercise B-8

Cash Proceeds from Bond

Exercise B-9

Present Value of Investment

Appendix B Exercise B-10 **Name** ____________________

(1)

(2)

Exercise B-11

Amount Borrowed

Exercise B-12

	Single Future Payment	Number of Periods	Interest Rate	Table B.1 Value	Amount Borrowed
(a)					
(b)					
(c)					
(d)					
(e)					
(f)					

Appendix B Exercise B-13 *Name* ____________________

(1) First Annuity:

Second Annuity:

(2) First Annuity:

Second Annuity:

Exercise B-14

(1) Present Value of Annuity

(2) Present Value of Annuity

(3) Present Value of Annuity

 Exercise B-15 *Name* ______

Total Accumulated in the Account

Exercise B-16

Total Accumulated in the Account

Exercise B-17

Future Value of the Fund

Exercise B-18

Future Value of Investment

Exercise B-19

	Present or Future Value	*Single Amount or Annuity*	*Relevant Table*	*Interest Rate*	*Number of Periods*
(a)					
(b)					
(c)					
(d)					

Appendix C Quick Study C-1 *Name* ____________________

GENERAL JOURNAL

Date		Account Titles and Explanation	P. R.	Debit	Credit

Quick Study C-2

(1) GENERAL JOURNAL

Date		Account Titles and Explanation	P. R.	Debit	Credit

(2)

(3) GENERAL JOURNAL

Date		Account Titles and Explanation	P. R.	Debit	Credit

Appendix C Quick Study C-3 *Name* ____________________________________

GENERAL JOURNAL

Date		Account Titles and Explanation	P. R.	Debit	Credit

Quick Study C-4

GENERAL JOURNAL

Date		Account Titles and Explanation	P. R.	Debit	Credit

Appendix C Quick Study C-5 *Name* ______________________________

True: ____

____

____

Quick Study C-6

(1) ____________________ (4) ____________________

(2) ____________________ (5) ____________________

(3) ____________________

Quick Study C-7

GENERAL JOURNAL

Date		Account Titles and Explanation	P. R.	Debit	Credit

Quick Study C-8

GENERAL JOURNAL

Date		Account Titles and Explanation	P. R.	Debit	Credit

 Quick Study C-9 *Name* ______________________

GENERAL JOURNAL

Date		Account Titles and Explanation	P. R.	Debit	Credit

Quick Study C-10

(1)

GENERAL JOURNAL

Date		Account Titles and Explanation	P. R.	Debit	Credit

(2)

Appendix C Quick Study C-11 *Name* ______________________

Quick Study C-12

Quick Study C-13[A] *Name* ______________________________

GENERAL JOURNAL

Date		Account Titles and Explanation	P. R.	Debit	Credit
		Date of Sale:			
		Date of Payment:			

Quick Study C-14[A]

GENERAL JOURNAL

Date		Account Titles and Explanation	P. R.	Debit	Credit

Appendix C **Exercise C-1** ***Name*** ______________________________

GENERAL JOURNAL

Date		Account Titles and Explanation	P. R.	Debit	Credit

 Exercise C-2 *Name* ______________________________

(1) GENERAL JOURNAL

Date		Account Titles and Explanation	P. R.	Debit	Credit

(2)

(3) GENERAL JOURNAL

Date		Account Titles and Explanation	P. R.	Debit	Credit

Exercise C-3

Available-for-Sale Portfolio	Cost	Market	Unrealized Gain (Loss)

GENERAL JOURNAL

Date		Account Titles and Explanation	P. R.	Debit	Credit

 Name ______________________________

GENERAL JOURNAL

Date		Account Titles and Explanation	P. R.	Debit	Credit

Appendix C Exercise C-5 *Name* ______________________________

GENERAL JOURNAL

Date		Account Titles and Explanation	P. R.	Debit	Credit

Computation of Market Adjustment:

Securities	Cost	Market	Unrealized Gain (Loss)

Exercise C-6

GENERAL JOURNAL

Date		Account Titles and Explanation	P. R.	Debit	Credit

Computation of Market Adjustment:

	12/31/2004	12/31/2005
Cost		
Market		
Gain (Loss)		

 Name ______________________________

GENERAL JOURNAL

Date		Account Titles and Explanation	P. R.	Debit	Credit
2003:					
2004:					
2005:					
2006:					

Supporting Computations:

Appendix C Exercise C-8 *Name* ______________________________

(a)

(b)

(c)

(d)

(e)

GENERAL JOURNAL

Date		Account Titles and Explanation	P. R.	Debit	Credit

Computation of Market Adjustment:

Long-Term AFS Securities	Cost	Market

 Name ______________________________

GENERAL JOURNAL

Date		Account Titles and Explanation	P. R.	Debit	Credit
2005:					
2006:					

 Name ______________________________

2005 Return on Total Assets:

2006 Return on Total Assets:

Analysis and Interpretation:

Appendix C Exercise C-11[A] *Name* ____________________

GENERAL JOURNAL

Date		Account Titles and Explanation	P. R.	Debit	Credit
2005:					
2006:					

 Name ____________________

Reported on Quarterly Statement Ended June 30, 2005:

Reported on Quarterly Statement Ended September 30, 2005:

Reported on Quarterly Statement Ended December 31, 2005:

Reported on Quarterly Statement Ended March 31, 2006:

 Name ______________________________

GENERAL JOURNAL

Date		Account Titles and Explanation	P. R.	Debit	Credit
2005:					
2006:					

Appendix C Problem C-1A or C-1B *Name* ______________________________
Part 1 (Continued)

GENERAL JOURNAL

Date		Account Titles and Explanation	P. R.	Debit	Credit
2007:					

Part 2

Date		Account Titles and Explanation	P. R.	Debit	Credit

Appendix C   Problem C-2A or C-2B   *Name* ______________________

Part 1

GENERAL JOURNAL

Date		Account Titles and Explanation	P. R.	Debit	Credit

Comparison of Cost and Market Values for AFS Portfolio

Security	Computations	Cost	Market	Unrealized Gain (Loss)

Part 3

GENERAL JOURNAL

Date		Account Titles and Explanation	P. R.	Debit	Credit

Part 4

Part 5

Income Statement

Balance Sheet (Equity Section):

Appendix C Problem C-3A or C-3B *Name* ______________________

Part 1

GENERAL JOURNAL

Date		Account Titles and Explanation	P. R.	Debit	Credit
2005:					

Supporting work:

GENERAL JOURNAL

Date		Account Titles and Explanation	P. R.	Debit	Credit
2006:					

Supporting work:

Appendix C Problem C-3A or C-3B *Name* ____________________

Part 1 (Continued)

GENERAL JOURNAL

Date		Account Titles and Explanation	P. R.	Debit	Credit
2007:					

Supporting work:

	12/31/2005	12/31/2006	12/31/2007
Long-Term AFS Securities (cost)			
Market Adjustment			
Long-Term AFS Securities (market)			

Part 3

	2005	2006	2007
Realized Gains (Losses)			
Unrealized Gains (Losses) at year-end*			

Problem C-4A or C-4B

Part 1

Balance sheet disclosure:

Supporting work:

AFS Securities on Dec. 31, 2005	Cost	Market

Appendix C Problem C-4A or C-4B Name ______________________
Part 2 (Continued)

GENERAL JOURNAL

Date		Account Titles and Explanation	P. R.	Debit	Credit

Supporting Computations:

AFS Securities	Cost	Market

Part 3

Stock Sold	Cost	Sale Price	Realized Gain (Loss)

Appendix C Problem C-5A or C-5B *Name* ______________________

Part 1

GENERAL JOURNAL

Date		Account Titles and Explanation	P. R.	Debit	Credit
2005:					
2006:					
2007:					

Name ______________________

(2) Carrying Value Per Share:

(3) Change in Equity:

Appendix C Part 2 Problem C-5A or C-5B (Continued) *Name* ______________________

(1)

GENERAL JOURNAL

Date		Account Titles and Explanation	P. R.	Debit	Credit
2005:					
2006:					
2007:					

(2) Investment Cost Per Share:

(3) Change in Equity:

Appendix C Problem C-6A[A] or C-6B[A] *Name* ______________________

Part 1

GENERAL JOURNAL

Date		Account Titles and Explanation	P. R.	Debit	Credit
2005:					

Appendix C Problem C-6A^A or C-6B^A *Name* ______________________

Part 1 (Continued)

GENERAL JOURNAL

Date		Account Titles and Explanation	P. R.	Debit	Credit
2006:					

Part 2

Foreign Exchange Gain (Loss) Reported:

Part 3

Appendix C Serial Problem Name ____________________
Success Systems

Part 1

GENERAL JOURNAL

Date		Account Titles and Explanation	P. R.	Debit	Credit

Part 2

GENERAL JOURNAL

Date		Account Titles and Explanation	P. R.	Debit	Credit

 Name ______________________________

BTN C-1

(1) ______________________________

(2) ______________________________

(3) ______________________________

(4) ______________________________

(5) Roll On: ______________________________

Appendix C Comparative Analysis *Name* ______________________
BTN 15-2

(1) Krispy Kreme's Return on Total Assets:

Current Year

Prior Year

Tastykake's Return on Total Assets:

Current Year

Prior Year

(2) Krispy Kreme's Component Analysis of Return on Total Assets:

Current Year

Prior Year

Tastykake's Component Analysis of Return on Total Assets:

Current Year

Prior Year

(3) Current Year Analysis:

Prior Year Analysis::

Appendix C Ethics Challenge **Name** ______________________

BTN C-5

(1) ______________________

(2) ______________________

(3) ______________________

MEMORANDUM

TO:
FROM:
DATE:
SUBJECT:

Appendix C Taking It to the Net **Name** ____________________

BTN C-5

(1)

(2)

(3)

(4)

 Business Week Activity ***Name*** ______________________

BTN 15-7

(1) ______________________

(2) ______________________

(3) (a) ______________________

(b) ______________________

(c) ______________________

(4) ______________________

(5) ______________________

 Entrepreneurial Decision *Name* ______________
BTN C-8

(1)

(2)

(3)

Hitting the Road--BTN C-9

(1)

(2)

(3)

 Name ______________________

(1) Grupo Bimbo's Return on Total Assets:

Current Year

Prior Year

(2) Grupo Bimbo's Component Analysis of Return on Total Assets:

Current Year

Prior Year

(3) Current Year Analysis:

Prior Year Analysis:

Overall:

Appendix D Quick Study D-1 *Name* ______________________

(a)

(b)

Quick Study D-2

	Share to Keeley	*Share to Norton*	*Total*
Net income			
Salary allowance:			
Keeley			
Norton			
Total salary allowances			
Balance of income			
Balance allocated:			
Keeley			
Norton			
Total allocated			
Balance of income			
Shares of the partners			

Quick Study D-3

Quick Study D-4

Appendix D Quick Study D-5 *Name* ______________________

GENERAL JOURNAL

Date		Account Titles and Explanation	P. R.	Debit	Credit

Quick Study D-6

GENERAL JOURNAL

Date		Account Titles and Explanation	P. R.	Debit	Credit

Quick Study D-7

Appendix D Exercise D-1 *Name* ______________________________

	Characteristic	General Partnerships
1.	Life	
2.	Owners' liability	
3.	Legal status	
4.	Tax status of income	
5.	Owners' authority	
6.	Ease of formation	
7.	Transferability of ownership	
8.	Ability to raise large amounts of capital	

Exercise D-2
Part a

Recommended Organization:

Taxation Effects:

Advantages:

Appendix D Exercise D-2 *Name* ______________________

Part b

Recommended Organization:

Taxation Effects:

Advantages:

Part c

Recommended Organization:

Taxation Effects:

Advantages:

Appendix D Exercise D-3 *Name* ______________________

(1)

GENERAL JOURNAL

Date		Account Titles and Explanation	P. R.	Debit	Credit

(2)

Capital account balances:	*Abbey*	*Adams*
Initial investment		
Withdrawals		
Share of income		
Ending balances		

 Name ______________________

Supporting calculations for (2)

Exercise D-4

	Share to Cosmo	*Share to Ellis*	*Total*
(1)			
(2)			
(3)			

 Exercise D-5 Name ______________________

	Share to Cosmo	Share to Ellis	Total
(1)			
(2)			

Exercise D-6

GENERAL JOURNAL

Date		Account Titles and Explanation	P. R.	Debit	Credit

Appendix D   Exercise D-7   *Name* ________________________________

(1)

GENERAL JOURNAL

Date		Account Titles and Explanation	P. R.	Debit	Credit

(2)

GENERAL JOURNAL

Date		Account Titles and Explanation	P. R.	Debit	Credit

(3)

GENERAL JOURNAL

Date		Account Titles and Explanation	P. R.	Debit	Credit

Appendix D Exercise D-8 *Name* ______________________

(1)

GENERAL JOURNAL

Date		Account Titles and Explanation	P. R.	Debit	Credit

(2)

GENERAL JOURNAL

Date		Account Titles and Explanation	P. R.	Debit	Credit

(3)

GENERAL JOURNAL

Date		Account Titles and Explanation	P. R.	Debit	Credit

Appendix D Exercise D-9 *Name* ______________________

(1)

	Red	White	Blue	Total
Initial investments				
Allocation of all losses				
Capital balances				

(2)

GENERAL JOURNAL

Date		Account Titles and Explanation	P. R.	Debit	Credit

(3)

GENERAL JOURNAL

Date		Account Titles and Explanation	P. R.	Debit	Credit

Appendix D Exercise D-10 *Name* ____________________

(a) Loss computation from selling assets:

(b) Loss allocation

	Tuttle	*Ritter*	*Lee*	*Total*
Capital balance before loss liquidation......................				
Allocation of loss:				
Capital balances after loss............				

(c) Liability to be paid:

Appendix D Exercise 12-11 *Name* ______________________

(a) Loss computation from selling assets:

(b) Loss and deficit allocation:

	Tuttle	*Ritter*	*Lee*	*Total*
Capital balance before loss.........				
Allocation of loss:				
Capital balances after loss...........				
Allocation of ________ deficit to				
Cash paid by each partner...........				

(c) Liability to be paid:

Exercise D-12

GENERAL JOURNAL

Date		Account Titles and Explanation	P. R.	Debit	Credit
(1)					
(2)					
(3)					

Supporting calculations:

Appendix D Problem D-2A or D-2B *Name* ____________________

Inc./Loss Sharing Plan	*Year 1* Calculations		
(a)			
(b)			
(c)			
(d)			

Inc./Loss Sharing Plan	*Year 2* Calculations		
(a)			
(b)			
(c)			
(d)			

Appendix D Problem D-2A or D-2B *Name* ______________________
(Continued)

Inc./Loss Sharing Plan	Calculations	*Year 3*	
(a)			
(b)			
(c)			
(d)			

Supporting Work Space:

Appendix D Problem D-3A or D-3B *Name* ______________________

Part 1

Inc./Loss Sharing Plan	Calculations				*Total*
(a)					
(b)					
(c)					

Appendix D Problem D-3A or D-3B *Name* ______________________________

Part 2 (Continued)

______________ PARTNERSHIP Statement of Partners' Equity For Year Ended December 31	________	________	________	*Total*
Beg. capital balances				
Plus:				
Owner investments				
Net Income:				
Salary allowances				
Interest allowances				
Balance allocated				
Total net income				
Total				
Less partners' withdrawals				
End. capital balances				

Part 3

GENERAL JOURNAL

Date		Account Titles and Explanation	P. R.	Debit	Credit

Appendix D Problem D-4A or D-4B *Name* ____________________

Part 1

GENERAL JOURNAL

Date		Account Titles and Explanation	P. R.	Debit	Credit
(a)					
(b)					
(c)					
(d)					
(e)					

Appendix D Problem D-4A or D-4B *Name* ____________________
Part 2 (Continued)

GENERAL JOURNAL

Date		Account Titles and Explanation	P. R.	Debit	Credit
(a)					
(b)					
(c)					

Appendix D Problem D-5A or D-5B *Name* ______________________

(1)

GENERAL JOURNAL

Date		Account Titles and Explanation	P. R.	Debit	Credit

Appendix D Problem D-5A or D-5B *Name* ______________________________
(Continued)

(2)

GENERAL JOURNAL

Date		Account Titles and Explanation	P. R.	Debit	Credit

Appendix D Problem D-5A or D-5B *Name* ______________________

(Continued)

(3)

GENERAL JOURNAL

Date		Account Titles and Explanation	P. R.	Debit	Credit

Appendix D Problem D-5A or D-5B *Name* ______________________________

(Continued)

(4)

GENERAL JOURNAL

Date		Account Titles and Explanation	P. R.	Debit	Credit

Appendix D Reporting in Action--BTN D-1 *Name* ______________________

(1)

(2)

(3)

Comparative Analysis--BTN D-2

(1)

(2)

(3)

(4)

(5)

Appendix D Ethics Challenge--BTN D-3 *Name* ______________________

(1) Income allocation per original agreement:

	Maben	Orlando	Clark	Total
Salary allowance				
Per patient charges				
Totals				

(2) Income allocation per Clark's proposal:

	Maben	Orlando	Clark	Total
Per patient charges				

(3)

 Name ______________________

STUDY NOTES
Organizations with Partnership Characteristics

Appendix D Taking It to the Net *Name* ______________________

BTN 12-5

(1)

(2)

(3)

(4)

Appendix D Teamwork in Action **BTN 12-6** *Name* ______________

(1)

Income/Loss Sharing Plan	Calculations	Baker	Warner	Rice	Total
(a)					
(b)					
(c)					
(d)					

(2) Team members share solutions.

(3)

Appendix D *Business Week* Activity *Name* ______________________

BTN 12-7

(1) ______________________

(2) ______________________

(3) ______________________

(4) ______________________

(5) ______________________

Entrepreneurial Decision--BTN D-8

(1) ______________________

(2) ______________________

(3) ______________________

 Name ______________________

(1) ______________________

____

____

(2) ______________________

____

____

(3) ______________________

____

____

____

(4) ______________________

____

(5) ______________________

____

____

Appendix E Quick Study E-1 *Name* ______________________

(1) ______________________
(2) ______________________
(3) ______________________
(4) ______________________
(5) ______________________

Quick Study E-2

(1) ______________________
(2) ______________________
(3) ______________________
(4) ______________________

Quick Study E-3

(1)	(7)
(2)	(8)
(3)	(9)
(4)	(10)
(5)	(11)
(6)	(12)

Quick Study E-4

(a) ______________________
(b) ______________________
(c) ______________________
(d) ______________________
(e) ______________________
(f) ______________________
(g) ______________________
(h) ______________________

 Quick Study E-5 *Name* ______________________________

GENERAL JOURNAL

Date		Account Titles and Explanation	P. R.	Debit	Credit

Quick Study E-6

Information Reportable:

____

____

____

____

Exercise E-1

SALES JOURNAL					
Date	Account Debited	Invoice Number	PR	Accts. Rec. Dr. Sales Cr.	Cost of Goods Sold Dr. Inventory Cr.

Exercise E-2

March 2 ______________________________

5 ______________________________

7 ______________________________

8 ______________________________

12 ______________________________

16 ______________________________

19 ______________________________

25 ______________________________

Appendix E Exercise E-3 *Name* ______________________

SALES JOURNAL				
Date	Account Debited	Invoice Number	PR	Accts. Rec. Dr. Sales Cr.

Exercise E-4

CASH RECEIPTS JOURNAL									
Date	Account Credited	Explanation	PR	Cash Dr.	Sales Discount Dr.	Accts. Rec. Cr.	Sales Cr.	Other Accts. Cr.	Cost of Goods Sold Dr. Inv. Cr.

Exercise E-5

November 3 ______________________

7 ______________________

9 ______________________

13 ______________________

18 ______________________

22 ______________________

27 ______________________

30 ______________________

Exercise E-6

CASH RECEIPTS JOURNAL								
Date	Account Credited	Explanation	PR	Cash Dr.	Sales Discount Dr.	Accts. Rec. Cr.	Sales Cr.	Other Accts. Cr.

 Exercise E-7 *Name* ______________________

PURCHASES JOURNAL								
Date	Account	Date of Invoice	Terms	PR	Accts. Payable Cr.	Inventory Dr.	Office Supplies Dr.	Other Accts. Dr.

Exercise E-8

June 1 ______________________
8 ______________________
14 ______________________
17 ______________________
24 ______________________
28 ______________________
29 ______________________

Exercise E-9

PURCHASES JOURNAL								
Date	Account	Date of Invoice	Terms	PR	Accts. Payable Cr.	Purchases Dr.	Office Supplies Dr.	Other Accts. Dr.

Exercise E-10

CASH DISBURSEMENTS JOURNAL								
Date	Ck. No.	Payee	Account Debited	PR	Cash Cr.	Inventory Cr.	Other Accts. Dr.	Accts. Payable Dr.

Appendix E Exercise E-11 *Name* ______________________

April 3
9
12
17
20
29
30
31

Exercise E-12

CASH DISBURSEMENTS JOURNAL								
Date	Ck. No.	Payee	Account Debited	PR	Cash Cr.	Purchases Discounts Cr.	Other Accts. Dr.	Accts. Payable Dr.

Exercise E-13

(a)

(b)

Appendix E Exercise E-14 *Name* ____________________

Part 1

ACCOUNTS RECEIVABLE SUBSIDIARY LEDGER

Anna Page	

Sara Reed	

Aaron Reckers	

Part 2

GENERAL LEDGER

Accounts Receivable	

Sales	

Sales Returns and Allowances	

Inventory	

Cost of Goods Sold	

Schedule of Accounts Receivable

Accounts Receivable Controlling Account

Appendix E Exercise E-15 *Name* ______________________________

Part 1

ACCOUNTS RECEIVABLE LEDGER

Eric Horner

Hong Jiang

Joe Mack

Tess Cox

Part 2

GENERAL LEDGER

Accounts Receivable

Sales

Part 3

Schedule of Accounts Receivable

Appendix E   Exercise E-16   *Name* ____________________

(1)

(2)

(3)

(4)

(5)

Exercise E-17

	Segment Income (in $ mil.)		Segment Assets (in %)		Segment Return on Assets
Segment	2004	2003	2004	2003	2004

Analysis and Interpretation:

Appendix E Problem E-1A or E-1B *Name* ______________________

Part 1

Sales Journal					Page 3
Date	Account Debited	Invoice Number	PR	Accts. Receivable Dr. Sales Cr.	Cost of Goods Sold Dr. Inventory Cr.

Cash Receipts Journal									Page 3
Date	Account Credited	Explanation	PR	Cash Dr.	Sales Disc. Dr.	Accts. Rec. Cr.	Sales Cr.	Other Accts. Cr.	Cost of Goods Sold Dr. Inv. Cr.

GENERAL LEDGER

Cash — **ACCOUNT NO. 101**

Date	Explanation	P.R.	DEBIT	CREDIT	BALANCE

Accounts Receivable — **ACCOUNT NO. 106**

Date	Explanation	P.R.	DEBIT	CREDIT	BALANCE

Inventory — **ACCOUNT NO. 119**

Date	Explanation	P.R.	DEBIT	CREDIT	BALANCE

Long-Term Notes Payable — **ACCOUNT NO. 251**

Date	Explanation	P.R.	DEBIT	CREDIT	BALANCE

Sales — **ACCOUNT NO. 413**

Date	Explanation	P.R.	DEBIT	CREDIT	BALANCE

Sales Discounts — **ACCOUNT NO. 415**

Date	Explanation	P.R.	DEBIT	CREDIT	BALANCE

Appendix E Problem E-1A or E-1B *Name* ______________________

Parts 2 & 3 (Continued)

Cost of Goods Sold ACCOUNT NO. 502

Date	Explanation	P.R.	DEBIT	CREDIT	BALANCE

ACCOUNTS RECEIVABLE LEDGER

Date	Explanation	P.R.	DEBIT	CREDIT	BALANCE

Date	Explanation	P.R.	DEBIT	CREDIT	BALANCE

Date	Explanation	P.R.	DEBIT	CREDIT	BALANCE

Appendix E Problem E-1A or E-1B *Name* ______________________

Parts 4 (Continued)

Trial Balance

Schedule of Accounts Receivable

Part 5

Analysis:

Appendix E Problem E-2A or E-2B *Name* ______________________
Parts 1 and 2

Sales Journal				Page 3
Date	Account Debited	Invoice Number	PR	Accts Receivable Dr. Sales Cr.

Cash Receipts Journal								Page 3
Date	Account Credited	Explanation	PR	Cash Dr.	Sales Discount Dr.	Accts. Rec. Cr.	Sales Cr.	Other Accts. Cr.

Appendix E Problem E-2A or E-2B *Name* ______________________
Parts 2 & 3 (Continued)

GENERAL LEDGER

Cash ACCOUNT NO. 101

Date	Explanation	P.R.	DEBIT	CREDIT	BALANCE

Accounts Receivable ACCOUNT NO. 106

Date	Explanation	P.R.	DEBIT	CREDIT	BALANCE

Inventory ACCOUNT NO. 119

Date	Explanation	P.R.	DEBIT	CREDIT	BALANCE

Long-Term Notes Payable ACCOUNT NO. 251

Date	Explanation	P.R.	DEBIT	CREDIT	BALANCE

Sales ACCOUNT NO. 413

Date	Explanation	P.R.	DEBIT	CREDIT	BALANCE

Sales Discounts ACCOUNT NO. 415

Date	Explanation	P.R.	DEBIT	CREDIT	BALANCE

Appendix E Problem E-2A or E-2B *Name* ______________________

Parts 2 & 3 (Continued)

ACCOUNTS RECEIVABLE LEDGER

Date	Explanation	P.R.	DEBIT	CREDIT	BALANCE

Date	Explanation	P.R.	DEBIT	CREDIT	BALANCE

Date	Explanation	P.R.	DEBIT	CREDIT	BALANCE

Trial Balance

Schedule of Accounts Receivable

Part 5

Analysis Component:

Appendix E Problem E-3A or E-3B *Name* ______________________

Parts 1 and 3

Purchases Journal								Page 3
Date	Account	Date of Invoice	Terms	PR	Accts. Payable Cr.	Inventory Dr.	Office Supplies Dr.	Other Accts. Dr.

Cash Disbursements Journal								Page 3
Date	Ck. No.	Payee	Account Debited	PR	Cash Cr.	Inventory Cr.	Other Accts. Dr.	Accts. Payable Dr.

GENERAL JOURNAL **Page 3**

Date		Account Titles and Explanation	P. R.	Debit	Credit

Appendix E Problem E-3A or E-3B *Name* ____________________

Parts 2 & 3 (Continued)

GENERAL LEDGER

Cash ACCOUNT NO. 101

Date	Explanation	P.R.	DEBIT	CREDIT	BALANCE

Inventory ACCOUNT NO. 119

Date	Explanation	P.R.	DEBIT	CREDIT	BALANCE

Office Supplies ACCOUNT NO. 124

Date	Explanation	P.R.	DEBIT	CREDIT	BALANCE

Store Supplies ACCOUNT NO. 125

Date	Explanation	P.R.	DEBIT	CREDIT	BALANCE

Store Equipment ACCOUNT NO. 165

Date	Explanation	P.R.	DEBIT	CREDIT	BALANCE

Accounts Payable ACCOUNT NO. 201

Date	Explanation	P.R.	DEBIT	CREDIT	BALANCE

Appendix E Problem E-3A or E-3B *Name* ______________________

Parts 2 & 3 (Continued)

Long-Term Notes Payable ACCOUNT NO. 251

Date	Explanation	P.R.	DEBIT	CREDIT	BALANCE

Sales Salaries Expense ACCOUNT NO. 621

Date	Explanation	P.R.	DEBIT	CREDIT	BALANCE

Advertising Expense ACCOUNT NO. 655

Date	Explanation	P.R.	DEBIT	CREDIT	BALANCE

ACCOUNTS PAYABLE LEDGER

Date	Explanation	P.R.	DEBIT	CREDIT	BALANCE

Date	Explanation	P.R.	DEBIT	CREDIT	BALANCE

Date	Explanation	P.R.	DEBIT	CREDIT	BALANCE

Appendix E Problem E-3A or E-3B *Name* ______________________

Parts 2 & 3 (Continued)

ACCOUNTS PAYABLE LEDGER

Date	Explanation	P.R.	DEBIT	CREDIT	BALANCE

Part 4

Trial Balance

Schedule of Accounts Payable

Appendix E Problem E-4A[A] or E-4B[A] *Name* ______________________

Parts 1 and 3 (Continued)

Purchases Journal								Page 3
Date	Account	Date of Invoice	Terms	PR	Accts. Payable Cr.	Purchases Dr.	Office Supplies Dr.	Other Accts. Dr.

Cash Disbursements Journal								Page 3
Date	Ck. No.	Payee	Account Debited	PR	Cash Cr.	Purchases Discount Cr.	Other Accts. Dr.	Accts. Payable Dr.

GENERAL JOURNAL **Page 3**

Date		Account Titles and Explanation	P. R.	Debit	Credit

Name ______________________

GENERAL LEDGER

Cash ACCOUNT NO. 101

Date	Explanation	P.R.	DEBIT	CREDIT	BALANCE

Inventory ACCOUNT NO. 119

Date	Explanation	P.R.	DEBIT	CREDIT	BALANCE

Office Supplies ACCOUNT NO. 124

Date	Explanation	P.R.	DEBIT	CREDIT	BALANCE

Store Supplies ACCOUNT NO. 125

Date	Explanation	P.R.	DEBIT	CREDIT	BALANCE

Store Equipment ACCOUNT NO. 165

Date	Explanation	P.R.	DEBIT	CREDIT	BALANCE

Accounts Payable ACCOUNT NO. 201

Date	Explanation	P.R.	DEBIT	CREDIT	BALANCE

Long-Term Notes Payable ACCOUNT NO. 251

Date	Explanation	P.R.	DEBIT	CREDIT	BALANCE

Purchases ACCOUNT NO. 505

Date	Explanation	P.R.	DEBIT	CREDIT	BALANCE

Purchase Returns and Allowances ACCOUNT NO. 506

Date	Explanation	P.R.	DEBIT	CREDIT	BALANCE

Purchase Discounts ACCOUNT NO. 507

Date	Explanation	P.R.	DEBIT	CREDIT	BALANCE

Sales Salaries Expense ACCOUNT NO. 621

Date	Explanation	P.R.	DEBIT	CREDIT	BALANCE

Advertising Expense ACCOUNT NO. 655

Date	Explanation	P.R.	DEBIT	CREDIT	BALANCE

Appendix E Problem E-4A or E-4B *Name* ______________________

Parts 2 & 3 (Continued)

ACCOUNTS PAYABLE LEDGER

____

Date	Explanation	P.R.	DEBIT	CREDIT	BALANCE

____

Date	Explanation	P.R.	DEBIT	CREDIT	BALANCE

____

Date	Explanation	P.R.	DEBIT	CREDIT	BALANCE

____

Date	Explanation	P.R.	DEBIT	CREDIT	BALANCE

Appendix E Problem E-4A or E-4B *Name* ____________

Part 3 (Continued)

Trial Balance

Schedule of Accounts Payable

Appendix E Problem E-5A or E-5B **Name** ______________________

Parts 1 and 2

Sales Journal					Page 2
Date	Account Debited	Invoice Number	PR	Accts. Rec. Dr. Sales Cr.	Cost of Goods Sold Dr. Inventory Cr.

Cash Receipts Journal									Page 2
Date	Account Credited	Explanation	PR	Cash Dr.	Sales Disc. Dr.	Accts. Rec. Cr.	Sales Cr.	Other Accts. Cr.	Cost of Goods Sold Dr. Inv. Cr.

Appendix E Problem E-5A or E-5B *Name* ____________________
Parts 1 and 2 (Continued)

Purchase Journal Page 2

Date	Account	Date of Inv.	Terms	PR	Accts. Pay. Cr.	Inventory Dr.	Office Supplies Dr.	Other Accts. Dr.

Cash Disbursements Journal Page 2

Date	Ck. No.	Payee	Account Debited	PR	Cash Cr.	Inventory Cr.	Other Accts. Dr.	Accts. Payable Dr.

GENERAL JOURNAL Page 2

Date		Account Titles and Explanation	P. R.	Debit	Credit

Appendix E Problem E-5A or E-5B *Name* ______________________

Parts 1 and 2 (Continued)

GENERAL LEDGER

Cash ACCOUNT NO. 101

Date	Explanation	P.R.	DEBIT	CREDIT	BALANCE

Accounts Receivable ACCOUNT NO. 106

Date	Explanation	P.R.	DEBIT	CREDIT	BALANCE

Inventory ACCOUNT NO. 119

Date	Explanation	P.R.	DEBIT	CREDIT	BALANCE

Office Supplies ACCOUNT NO. 124

Date	Explanation	P.R.	DEBIT	CREDIT	BALANCE

Store Supplies ACCOUNT NO. 125

Date	Explanation	P.R.	DEBIT	CREDIT	BALANCE

Office Equipment ACCOUNT NO. 163

Date	Explanation	P.R.	DEBIT	CREDIT	BALANCE

Appendix E Problem E-5A or E-5B *Name* ______________________

Parts 1 and 2 (Continued)

Accounts Payable — ACCOUNT NO. 201

Date	Explanation	P.R.	DEBIT	CREDIT	BALANCE

Long-Term Notes Payable — ACCOUNT NO. 251

Date	Explanation	P.R.	DEBIT	CREDIT	BALANCE

Common Stock — ACCOUNT NO. 307

Date	Explanation	P.R.	DEBIT	CREDIT	BALANCE

Retained Earnings — ACCOUNT NO. 318

Date	Explanation	P.R.	DEBIT	CREDIT	BALANCE

Sales — ACCOUNT NO. 413

Date	Explanation	P.R.	DEBIT	CREDIT	BALANCE

Sales Discounts — ACCOUNT NO. 415

Date	Explanation	P.R.	DEBIT	CREDIT	BALANCE

Cost of Goods Sold — ACCOUNT NO. 502

Date	Explanation	P.R.	DEBIT	CREDIT	BALANCE

Sales Salaries Expense ACCOUNT NO. 621

Date	Explanation	P.R.	DEBIT	CREDIT	BALANCE

ACCOUNTS RECEIVABLE LEDGER

Date	Explanation	P.R.	DEBIT	CREDIT	BALANCE

Date	Explanation	P.R.	DEBIT	CREDIT	BALANCE

Date	Explanation	P.R.	DEBIT	CREDIT	BALANCE

Appendix E Problem E-5A or E-5B *Name* ______________________________
Parts 1 and 2 (Continued)

ACCOUNTS PAYABLE LEDGER

____

Date	Explanation	P.R.	DEBIT	CREDIT	BALANCE

____

Date	Explanation	P.R.	DEBIT	CREDIT	BALANCE

____

Date	Explanation	P.R.	DEBIT	CREDIT	BALANCE

____

Date	Explanation	P.R.	DEBIT	CREDIT	BALANCE

Trial Balance

Schedule of Accounts Receivable

Schedule of Accounts Payable

Appendix E Problem E-6A or E-6B *Name* ______________________

Parts 1 and 2

Sales Journal				Page 2
Date	Account Debited	Invoice Number	PR	Accts. Receivable Dr. Sales Cr.

Cash Receipts Journal								Page 2
Date	Account Credited	Explanation	PR	Cash Dr.	Sales Disc. Dr.	Accts. Rec. Cr.	Sales Cr.	Other Accts. Cr.

Purchases Journal Page 2

Date	Account	Date of Inv.	Terms	PR	Accts. Payable Cr.	Purchases Dr.	Office Supplies Dr.	Other Accts. Dr.

Cash Disbursements Journal Page 2

Date	Ck. No.	Payee	Account Debited	PR	Cash Cr.	Purch. Disc. Cr.	Other Accts. Dr.	Accts. Payable Dr.

GENERAL JOURNAL Page 2

Date		Account Titles and Explanation	P. R.	Debit	Credit

Appendix E Problem E-6A or E-6B *Name* ____________________

Parts 1 and 2 (Continued)

GENERAL LEDGER

Cash ACCOUNT NO. 101

Date	Explanation	P.R.	DEBIT	CREDIT	BALANCE

Accounts Receivable ACCOUNT NO. 106

Date	Explanation	P.R.	DEBIT	CREDIT	BALANCE

Inventory ACCOUNT NO. 119

Date	Explanation	P.R.	DEBIT	CREDIT	BALANCE

Office Supplies ACCOUNT NO. 124

Date	Explanation	P.R.	DEBIT	CREDIT	BALANCE

Store Supplies ACCOUNT NO. 125

Date	Explanation	P.R.	DEBIT	CREDIT	BALANCE

Office Equipment ACCOUNT NO. 163

Date	Explanation	P.R.	DEBIT	CREDIT	BALANCE

Appendix E Problem E-6A or E-6B *Name* ______________________

Parts 1 and 2 (Continued)

Accounts Payable ACCOUNT NO. 201

Date	Explanation	P.R.	DEBIT	CREDIT	BALANCE

Long-Term Notes Payable ACCOUNT NO. 251

Date	Explanation	P.R.	DEBIT	CREDIT	BALANCE

Common Stock ACCOUNT NO. 307

Date	Explanation	P.R.	DEBIT	CREDIT	BALANCE

Retained Earnings ACCOUNT NO. 318

Date	Explanation	P.R.	DEBIT	CREDIT	BALANCE

Sales ACCOUNT NO. 413

Date	Explanation	P.R.	DEBIT	CREDIT	BALANCE

Sales Discounts ACCOUNT NO. 415

Date	Explanation	P.R.	DEBIT	CREDIT	BALANCE

Purchases ACCOUNT NO. 505

Date	Explanation	P.R.	DEBIT	CREDIT	BALANCE

Appendix E Problem E-6A or E-6B *Name* ______________________

Parts 1 and 2 (Continued)

Purchases Returns and Allowances **ACCOUNT NO. 506**

Date	Explanation	P.R.	DEBIT	CREDIT	BALANCE

Purchases Discount **ACCOUNT NO. 507**

Date	Explanation	P.R.	DEBIT	CREDIT	BALANCE

Sales Salaries Expense **ACCOUNT NO. 621**

Date	Explanation	P.R.	DEBIT	CREDIT	BALANCE

ACCOUNTS RECEIVABLE LEDGER

Date	Explanation	P.R.	DEBIT	CREDIT	BALANCE

Date	Explanation	P.R.	DEBIT	CREDIT	BALANCE

Date	Explanation	P.R.	DEBIT	CREDIT	BALANCE

Appendix E Problem E-6A or E-6B *Name* ______________________

Parts 1 and 2 (Continued)

ACCOUNTS PAYABLE LEDGER

Date	Explanation	P.R.	DEBIT	CREDIT	BALANCE

Date	Explanation	P.R.	DEBIT	CREDIT	BALANCE

Date	Explanation	P.R.	DEBIT	CREDIT	BALANCE

Date	Explanation	P.R.	DEBIT	CREDIT	BALANCE

Trial Balance

Schedule of Accounts Receivable

Schedule of Accounts Payable

Appendix E Reporting in Action--BTN E-1 *Name* ______________________

(1)

(2)

(3) Roll On:

Appendix E Comparative Analysis *Name* ______________________
BTN E-2

Parts 1 and 2 Computations

Segment	% Change	Current	% Change	One Year Prior	Two Years Prior

(1) Part 1 Interpretation: ______________________

(2) Part 2 Interpretation: ______________________

 Name ____________________

(1)

(2)

(3)

 Name ____________________

MEMORANDUM

TO:
FROM:
SUBJECT:
DATE:

Appendix E Taking It to the Net--BTN E-5 *Name* ______________________

(1)

(2)

(3)

(4)

Appendix E Teamwork In Action--BTN E-6 *Name* ______________________

Parts 1 and 2

SALES JOURNAL					Page 2
Date	Account Debited	Invoice Number	PR	Accts. Rec. Dr. Sales Cr.	Cost of Goods Sold Dr. Inventory Cr.

Cash Receipts Journal									
Date	Account Credited	Explanation	PR	Cash Dr.	Sales Disc. Dr.	Accts. Rec. Cr.	Sales Cr.	Other Accts. Cr.	Cost of Goods Sold Dr. Inv. Cr.

Purchases Journal									Page 2
Date		Account	Date of Invoice	Terms	PR	Accts. Payable Cr.	Inventory Dr.	Office Supplies Dr.	Other Accts. Dr.

Cash Disbursements Journal								Page 2
Date	Ck. No.	Payee	Account Debited	PR	Cash Cr.	Inventory Cr.	Other Accts. Dr.	Accts. Payable Dr.

GENERAL JOURNAL Page 2

Date		Account Titles and Explanation	P.R.	Debit	Credit

GENERAL LEDGER

Cash — **ACCOUNT NO. 101**

Date	Explanation	P.R.	DEBIT	CREDIT	BALANCE

Accounts Receivable — **ACCOUNT NO. 106**

Date	Explanation	P.R.	DEBIT	CREDIT	BALANCE

Inventory — **ACCOUNT NO. 119**

Date	Explanation	P.R.	DEBIT	CREDIT	BALANCE

Office Supplies — **ACCOUNT NO. 124**

Date	Explanation	P.R.	DEBIT	CREDIT	BALANCE

Store Supplies — **ACCOUNT NO. 125**

Date	Explanation	P.R.	DEBIT	CREDIT	BALANCE

Office Equipment — **ACCOUNT NO. 163**

Date	Explanation	P.R.	DEBIT	CREDIT	BALANCE

 Name ______________________________

Accounts Payable ACCOUNT NO. 201

Date	Explanation	P.R.	DEBIT	CREDIT	BALANCE

Long-Term Notes Payable ACCOUNT NO. 251

Date	Explanation	P.R.	DEBIT	CREDIT	BALANCE

Common Stock ACCOUNT NO. 307

Date	Explanation	P.R.	DEBIT	CREDIT	BALANCE

Retained Earnings ACCOUNT NO. 318

Date	Explanation	P.R.	DEBIT	CREDIT	BALANCE

Sales ACCOUNT NO. 413

Date	Explanation	P.R.	DEBIT	CREDIT	BALANCE

Sales Discounts ACCOUNT NO. 415

Date	Explanation	P.R.	DEBIT	CREDIT	BALANCE

Cost of Goods Sold ACCOUNT NO. 502

Date	Explanation	P.R.	DEBIT	CREDIT	BALANCE

Sales Salaries Expense ACCOUNT NO. 621

Date	Explanation	P.R.	DEBIT	CREDIT	BALANCE

ACCOUNTS RECEIVABLE LEDGER

Date	Explanation	P.R.	DEBIT	CREDIT	BALANCE

Date	Explanation	P.R.	DEBIT	CREDIT	BALANCE

Date	Explanation	P.R.	DEBIT	CREDIT	BALANCE

ACCOUNTS PAYABLE LEDGER

Date	Explanation	P.R.	DEBIT	CREDIT	BALANCE

Date	Explanation	P.R.	DEBIT	CREDIT	BALANCE

Date	Explanation	P.R.	DEBIT	CREDIT	BALANCE

Date	Explanation	P.R.	DEBIT	CREDIT	BALANCE

Trial Balance

Schedule of Accounts Receivable

Schedule of Accounts Payable

 Name ______________________

BTN E-7

(1)

(2)

(3)

(4)

Appendix E Entrepreneurial Decision *Name* ______________________

BTN E-8

(1)

(2)

(3)

Appendix E Global Decision--BTN E-9 *Name* ______________________

(1) ______________________

____

____

(2) ______________________

____

____

(3) ______________________

____

____

(4) ______________________

____

____